*From Brooklyn to Benares
and Back*

From Brooklyn to Benares and Back

Dada Vedaprajinananda

InnerWorld Publications
San Germán, Puerto Rico
www.innerworldpublications.com

Copyright © 2015 by Dada Vedaprajinananda

All rights reserved under International and Pan-American Copyright Conventions. Published in the United States by InnerWorld Publications, PO Box 1613, San Germán, Puerto Rico, 00683.

Library of Congress Control Number: 2014920099

Cover Design: Mukti Lourdes Sanchez

Back cover photo: Gary Warnimont

No part of this book may be reproduced or transmitted in any form or by any means, electronic or mechanical, including photocopying, recording, or by any information storage or retrieval system, without permission in writing from the publisher, except for the inclusion of brief quotations in a review.

ISBN: 9781881717379

To the Cosmic Magician

Preface

How does a boy from Brooklyn end up as an orange-clad yogic monk? That's the story I want to tell, not only to satisfy the curiosity of people who stare at me and wonder "What makes this guy tick?" but also in hopes of encouraging others to walk on the spiritual path.

I recognize that there are a few different types of readers who might want to read this book. Since I am a disciple of a guru, Shrii Shrii Anandamurti, I know that there are other co-disciples who will be interested in my recollections of my time with our teacher. My description of events in India and also in Switzerland and France include many incidents with Anandamurti that have never been recorded before. Other readers may be interested to find out how an American, growing up in the 1950s and 1960s, turned to the path of Eastern spirituality and ended up traveling around the world as a yoga and meditation teacher. I have tried to strike a balance so that both people who are already familiar with the Ananda Marga spiritual path and those who are encountering it for the first time, in the form of my narrative, will find the book meaningful.

I didn't keep a journal during the years described here, so there are undoubtedly some errors regarding dates. Also, I have been very selective about what I have written about and what has been left out. I have concentrated on my years as a yogi and a monk because it was this period in which I encountered the ideas and practices that I feel are so important to share with others.

1

From Brooklyn to California

IN THE SUMMER of 1946, while much of the rest of the world had been shattered by the Second World War, America was entering a boom period. It was a high-water mark for Brooklyn and New York City, a time before many of the problems that currently blight urban America became so pronounced. It was not a perfect era but it was a time of optimism. Here, on a tree-lined street in a section of Brooklyn known as East Flatbush, I spent my first nine years.

One of the first things that Americans did after World War II was to buy new cars. The new cars were influenced by a fascination with the aviation industry. My father bought a 1950 Studebaker. People used to make fun of its aerodynamic shape and its rear wrap-around windows, which resembled an airplane cockpit, saying, "We don't know if it is coming or going." With its propeller-like pointed nose, this particular model was one of the icons of the era.

At the end of the decade my family bought a 1960 Plymouth, which didn't have a propeller but did sport giant tail-fins.

Television, which was developed in the late 1920s, also came on in a big way after the War. Sometime in 1949 my father came home with a television set. With a TV in our own living room, a new world of entertainment opened up for us. One of my early favorite TV shows was "Captain Video." It was a crazy mixture of science fiction with occasional, incongruous clips from Westerns blended in. I was too young to mind the inexplicable scene changes and loved the sequences where *The Galaxy*, Captain Video's spaceship, soared through the stars accompanied by dramatic classical music.

We watched lots of Westerns, including old movies featuring the singing cowboy Gene Autry, as well as episodes of several series that were created for television such as *The Cisco Kid* and *The Lone Ranger*, which first aired in 1949. New children's shows also appeared. The most popular kids' program was *The Howdy Doody Show* in which the actor "Buffalo" Bob Smith, dressed in Western clothing, and an array of other actors, puppets, and marionettes, including the freckle-faced star of the program, kept us glued to the TV set. *The Howdy Doody Show* was broadcast from New York City with a live studio audience and a special children's section known as "the peanut gallery." I never made it to the peanut gallery, but one day in the early 1950s, my mother took me to Manhattan and I became part of the audience of Howdy Doody's main rival, Rootie Kazootie. This was a similar program with a puppet as the main character and human co-stars. We sat in Rootie Kazootie's equivalent of the peanut gallery and joined in singing the show's theme song with gusto: "Who is the boy, who is full of zip and joy? He's Rootie Kazootie!"

Rootie Kazootie

I didn't confine my TV viewing to children's shows. I enjoyed the many variety shows that had heavy doses of sketch and stand-up comedy. Milton Berle, Red Skelton, Jack Benny, Groucho Marx and Jackie Gleason were some of the TV pioneers, but I think the most amazing entertainer of that era was Sid Caesar, who could contort his face in any way necessary to get us to laugh.

While Sid Caesar—backed by stellar writers such as Mel Brooks, Carl Reiner and Woody Allen—had to go through a whole routine to get his laughs, I noticed that the stand-up comics only had to go out on stage and say one word, "Brooklyn," and everyone would start laughing. I never quite understood what was so funny about my hometown, but it was an automatic hit for the comedians of that era.

This period was not all fun and laughs, however. Serious events were happening around the world and even a young boy like me took notice. In March 1953 someone told me that Josef Stalin had died. I had no idea who he was but as I got older, I began to understand the importance of events like this.

I watched the coronation of Queen Elizabeth on television in June, 1953. The coronation was the world's first major international event to be broadcast on television. By that time I knew that a carnation was a flower, but I didn't really understand what a coronation was. I watched as the young queen was transported to the palace in a gilded, horse-drawn carriage, not knowing that in 1966 I would be on the streets of London watching the Queen's carriage roll by with President Ayub Kahn of Pakistan sitting beside her.

Just a month after the coronation of Queen Elizabeth, I saw the front page of a tabloid New York newspaper with a big photo of grimy-faced soldiers and a headline announcing the end of the Korean War. I had hardly been aware of the war because I was so young and the war was so far away. However, like all New York City children of that era, I had metal dog tags that were supposed to identify me in case of an attack on the US.

In 1954 I glanced at a cover of *Life Magazine* and saw a mushroom cloud on the cover. It was a picture of a US test of a huge fifteen-megaton hydrogen bomb in the South Pacific.

Though there were ominous events going on around the world, we also had plenty of diversions to keep us happy. Sometime in 1954 my aunt invited me on an excursion to Bear Mountain, a popular tourist and picnic location north of New York City. In those days, before everybody had automobiles, a popular way to make this trip was on large excursion boats that plied the Hudson River. The boat was packed with tourists of all ages, but it was the teenagers who made the most noise. A large group of them had spread out on a dance floor of the ship doing a frantic jitterbug to fast-tempo music coming out of a loudspeaker with these lyrics:

Go, go, go everybody
Go, go, go everybody
Go, go, go, go, go, go, go

I didn't know what it was at the time; it was one of the first hit recordings of rock 'n' roll music, Bill Haley's "Crazy Man Crazy." I would soon find out about rock 'n' roll because in 1955 this new style became the dominant form of American popular music. The ascendance of rock 'n' roll was marked by the sensational Elvis Presley who appeared on our TV sets on the popular variety shows in 1956. He belted out his hits shown only from the waist up because his body movements were deemed indecent by some critics. There was a lot of opposition to this new music, and many "experts" said that it wouldn't be around too long.

I was not sure if the critics were right or wrong about the longevity of rock 'n' roll but I listened to it quite a lot. I not only listened to it, I also went to some of the first rock 'n' roll concerts of the era, which were staged in downtown Brooklyn by Alan Freed. Freed was a Cleveland disc jockey credited with coining the term "rock 'n' roll." He used to gather the top acts of the day for concerts in major US cities. The concerts were usually held during school vacation periods and I went to his concerts during the Christmas vacation of 1958 and the Easter vacation of 1959.

Going to Alan Freed's "rock 'n' roll shows" was something of an adventure for me, because by this time I no longer lived in Brooklyn. Like many other American families, my family moved to the suburbs in 1955. We now lived on Long Island's south shore, about twenty-five miles east of Brooklyn. I would get up in the morning around 5:00 AM and go to Brooklyn with my father, who was a machinist in a factory in the easternmost section of Brooklyn. There I would meet my cousin Alan, who, though a bit younger than me, was the driving force behind these expeditions. We would get on the subway and go to the Paramount Theater in downtown Brooklyn. Though we would arrive before 8:00 AM, there were always long lines of youngsters already there, waiting for the theater to open.

We would wait patiently until the doors opened around noon and let us into the ornately decorated four-thousand-seat theater that had been constructed in 1928. The program opened with a movie, followed by a long concert featuring the top performers of the day. We received a large concert program featuring photos of all the stars. One of the most memorable acts I saw was a performance by Jackie Wilson in 1959. He was called "Mr. Excitement" and he didn't disappoint. He had an almost operatic voice and would jump from a standing singing position to his knees in a ballet-like split, all the while singing his heart out. I also saw one of the last performances of the Big Bopper, a singer who died along with Buddy Holly and Richie Valens in 1959.

Baseball also attracted my attention. The 1950s were a golden age for professional baseball in New York. One of the city's three teams—Dodgers, Giants, and Yankees— won championships in each of the years from 1949 through 1955. In the greater New York City area, fans were fiercely loyal to their chosen team. I grew up in Brooklyn and I should have rooted for the Brooklyn Dodgers, but sometime in 1953 an aunt said to me "Why root for the Dodgers, the Yankees beat them every year?" Indeed, the Yankees had defeated the Dodgers in 1941, 1947, 1949, 1951, 1952 and 1953 in baseball's championship tournament, which is known as the World Series, even though only teams from the US compete in it. As an impressionable seven year old, I did the unthinkable and switched my allegiance to the Yankees.

As I grew older, I got involved in the arguments with other New Yorkers about which of the center fielders of the New York teams—the Dodgers' Duke Snider, the Yankees' Mickey Mantle or the Giants' Willie Mays— was the better player. Each of them was great and eventually they were all voted into baseball's Hall of Fame. However, at the time we insisted that "our" center fielder was clearly the best. We watched a lot of games on TV or listened on the radio. Radiocasts of the World Series were even piped into our classrooms.

I didn't get to see a major league baseball game live until 1961, when I went with my cousin Alan to Yankee Stadium. Alan was a Giants fan but by this time the Giants and the Dodgers had left New York. Just like our trips to Alan Freed's rock 'n' roll shows, we reached the stadium early and waited outside, hoping to get a glimpse of some of the famous players as they entered the ballpark. We waited a short while and then a limousine pulled up and out came Mickey Mantle wearing a big cowboy hat. He flashed a smile at us and all the waiting fans, and then entered the stadium to do his work.

We too entered the stadium. I was amazed when we went through a dark tunnel and ramp and then after a few steps saw the brilliant green grass of this famous baseball field for the first time. We sat in the right field bleachers and watched as home runs hit by Mickey Mantle and his teammate Roger Maris sailed into the bullpen area just a few feet from us. That summer Mantle and Maris made headlines as they raced to beat the home run record set by Babe Ruth in 1927.

Not only were the great athletes on these teams huge heroes, but the coaches and managers were also colorful characters. The Yankees manager Casey Stengel provided almost as much entertainment off the field as his players did on the field. After the games he gave press conferences speaking in an almost unintelligible stream-of-conscious delivery that was dubbed "Stengelese" by the sports reporters who called him "The Old Professor."

In 1958 Casey Stengel took his unique style to the US Senate where he testified before the Anti-Trust and Monopoly Subcommittee. The Senate was trying to determine whether baseball should be exempted from laws that prevented the formation of trusts and monopolies. They sought Stengel's learned input but instead got treated to a wandering, hilarious forty-five minute discourse. He began by telling about his background:

"I had many years that I was not so successful as a ballplayer, as it is a game of skill. And then I was no doubt discharged by baseball in which I had to go back to the minor leagues as a manager, and after being in the minor leagues as a manager, I became a major league manager in several cities and was discharged, we call it 'discharged,' because there is no question I had to leave."

The Senators laughed and then asked questions about the possible worldwide expansion of baseball and were treated to more Stengelese.

"I made a tour overseas with the New York Yankees several years ago, and it was the most amazing tour I ever saw for a ball club, to go over where you have trouble spots. It wouldn't make any difference whether he was a Republican or Democrat, and so forth. I know that over there we drew 250,000 to 500,000 people in the streets, in which they stood in front of the automobiles, not on the sidewalks, and those people are trying to play baseball over there with short fingers and I say, 'Why do you do it?'"

I don't think the Senators, who asked questions about the future of baseball, got much out of Stengel's testimony. However, just to make sure, they asked Mickey Mantle, who accompanied his manager to the hearings, what his opinion was. He replied simply, "My views are about the same as Casey's."

Rock 'n' roll, TV, and baseball were fun, no doubt, but they couldn't hide the realization that a nuclear Sword of Damocles was hanging over us throughout this period. In 1957 the Russians launched Sputnik, the first artificial earth satellite, and the age of nuclear-tipped missiles pointed everywhere had arrived. In 1960 the Soviet Premier Nikita Khrushchev came to the US and scared the living daylights out of me and everyone else when he banged his shoe on the podium of the United Nations and then went on TV and declared, "Your grandchildren will live under Communism."

It got even worse when we watched television in October 1962 and saw President Kennedy explaining that the Soviet Union had placed nuclear-armed missiles in Cuba. We now know that the world came very close to a catastrophic war at that moment and I, along with everyone else living at that time, was fortunate that peace prevailed; however in the 1950s and the early part of the 1960s, we were not so sure that this would be the case. In 1956 I went to the movies and saw a film entitled *The Day the World Ended*, in which mutants terrorize the survivors of a nuclear attack. Later on, around 1960, I saw a more sophisticated film, an adaptation of Nevil Shute's novel *On the Beach*, depicting the last survivors of a nuclear war waiting for fallout to take its final toll. We knew that the fictional attack was set sometime in the near future, but when a fleeting view of a wall calendar revealed a 1964 date, everyone in the theater shuddered.

These were exciting and scary times in which to grow up, but they were just a preparation for what was to come next.

The Transition

My change from an ordinary adolescent into a spiritual seeker came about in a rather swift and unexpected way. This is the most difficult thing for me to write about or explain because there was nothing in my observable background that could serve as a predictor of my eventual vocation.

When I was young and people asked me what I wanted to be when I grew up, I never said, "I want to be a yogi." The only yogi that I knew about was a baseball player named Yogi Berra. And although he would later be acclaimed for his humorous, Zen-like sayings, he had nothing to do with yoga.

I really didn't know what I wanted to be or do in the future. I knew that I was keenly interested in current events but beyond this I was not sure what would come next. I did well academically in high school, and really did not have any deep religious or spiritual views in this period. In fact at one point, I thought that I was an atheist.

When I went to a liberal arts college in upstate New York, things started to change, gradually at first and then very quickly. I took a required class in philosophy and religion and was introduced to the works of existentialists,

Christian existentialists, Tolstoy, Plato and other thinkers. My outlook expanded due to this study and I soon became ready to accept a spiritual approach to life.

I had entered college with a social mindset heavily influenced by the simplistic social studies curriculum of high school. We had been led to believe, like students in every other country, that our country always did everything for the good of humanity. The US expanded from ocean to ocean because it was "Manifest Destiny" and meddled in the affairs of every Central American nation because we stood behind the "Monroe Doctrine," which somehow justified treating this area as a special sphere of interest. We never considered that what had happened to the Native Americans could be considered ethnic cleansing or genocide, or that maybe the Central Americans didn't really like our countless armed interventions.

Vietnam helped to change all of that. I remember attending a Bacchanalian induction to my college fraternity in February 1965 and one of the drunken frat brothers started to shout, "We're at war!" The US had just started bombing Hanoi in North Vietnam and the simmering war was about to become something very big. This was the first war to be broadcast live on TV each night. We students watched images of US soldiers igniting the huts of Vietnamese villagers with Zippo cigarette lighters and listened to a press conference where a US commander solemnly stated that "We had to destroy that village in order to save it."

The newscasters Walter Cronkite and Eric Sevareid, who brought us this news in a seemingly objective manner, were our heroes—we even selected Sevareid for an honorary degree given to him at our Colgate University graduation in 1968. My mind was definitely changing from exposure to the war in Vietnam.

This process continued in 1966 when I spent a half year in London as part of our college's overseas study program. I studied the British economy, but it was the exposure to the "Swinging London" of the Beatles that hastened my social awakening. When I returned to the US in January 1967 I was not the same young man who had entered college in September 1964.

I joined the anti-war demonstrations in upstate New York and even journeyed all the way to Washington, D.C., for a mammoth anti-war demonstration at the Pentagon in October 1967. That was the demonstration, described in Norman Mailer's book *Armies of the Night*, in which 35,000 young people surrounded the Pentagon, and Yippie leaders like Abbie Hoffman and the poet Allen Ginsberg attempted to "levitate" the Pentagon with chants of OM!

I was impressed by the bravery of the protesters who defied the rows of armed troops who were trying to protect the Pentagon. I also felt emboldened by the scene but I was not completely fearless and made sure I wasn't arrested. Still, spending the whole night outside in the demonstration and listening to folk songs and speeches had an inspiring effect on me.

Another important demonstration happened right on my college campus in April 1968. When shots were fired from a fraternity house at an African-American student, demonstrations by the college's black students began. The black students were joined by hundreds of white students demanding an end to discriminatory policies in the college's fraternities. The demonstrations culminated with a five-day sit-in the administration building. I took part in the occupation of the administration building, and once again the experience of being together with people struggling for an idealistic cause was exhilarating. When the demonstration was over, some people described it as a "religious experience."

The times were definitely changing and I was changing too. Like many of my peers, I began to experiment with drugs. I smoked marijuana and tried LSD. While I was doing these things, I was also reading books with spiritual content by Aldous Huxley, Alan Watts, and others. So I don't know which was the "chicken" or which was the "egg," or what was the real explanation for my transformed worldview, but after going through this experience, I became intensely interested in spirituality.

In my senior year of college I had to prepare for graduation and for life after graduation. I applied to graduate schools in the field of international relations and got a full fellowship to Columbia University, but my heart was no longer in conventional academic studies. I had been "radicalized" socially in large part due to the war in Vietnam and was now also yearning to expand my spiritual knowledge and experience.

Hitching to California, Morningstar Ranch, Lou Gottlieb

Sometime in the summer of 1968, I wanted to go to California to see what was happening there. I had heard about the "Summer of Love" of 1967 when the hippie sub-culture became well known and I was attracted to the visions of peace, love, and spiritual awakening associated with this movement.

I took leave from a menial summer job, bought a sleeping bag, and took a bus from New York to Washington, D.C., and then continued on to California, hitchhiking rides with a sign that simply read "California." It took around six days to reach Los Angeles, where I stayed with my cousin Alan, who was an aspiring rock musician.

My hair was growing longer, and I now had a mustache and the beginnings of a beard. I looked like I belonged in the West Coast hippie environment.

After some days in LA, I decided to go to Northern California and went out to the scenic Pacific Coast Highway, also known as Highway Number 1. I stuck out my thumb and was on my way. After passing through San Francisco and Sausalito, I reached a place in Sonoma County called Morningstar Ranch. It was a piece of land owned by a musician named Lou Gottlieb. Gottlieb had been a member of a famous folk group of the 1950s called The Limelighters, but by this time he had retired. He lived on this piece of land in a small cabin where he passed his time playing classical music on a piano.

The rest of his property was populated by hippies living in tents and tree houses. Naturally this irked Gottlieb's rural neighbors, who took him to court for violation of various zoning codes governing properties in that county. Gottlieb told us that when he was in court, he explained to the judge that he had given his land back to God and that anyone was free to come there and camp out on the property.

Gottlieb said that the judge then asked him which god he had given his property to, and he replied by taking out a dollar bill that said "In God We Trust." He pointed to the note and said "This God."

When I was there, the legal process was still going on but Gottlieb did manage to create a stir with this action. According to *Wikipedia*, a series of court appeals culminated in the Ninth District Court ruling that he could not deed his land to God. The ruling centered round the fact that if God was named owner on a quit claim deed, there would be no recourse for the collection of property taxes. The finding, therefore, was that God has no property rights in the state of California. An obituary for Gottlieb, who passed away in 1996, gave another explanation, saying that the judge denied Gottlieb's donation of his ranch to God because God would have to appear in person to accept the gift.

In any case, I stayed for a few days on the commune and met different people who shared what they knew about spirituality. One day, however, Gottlieb surprised me. We were near his cabin and he came out and said, "You hippies don't know what you are doing." This puzzled me because I thought that he, with his long hair and thick black beard, was "one of us." He continued, "You just hang out doing nothing but what you should really be doing is selfless service."

Selfless service — I don't even know if I had really heard of this concept before Gottlieb blurted it out to us, but very soon I was going to encounter a teacher who made this one of the pillars of his teaching.

Can I Recommend a Porsche?

After a short time at Morningstar Ranch, I headed back to Los Angeles. While I was in Los Angeles sometime in August 1968, I unexpectedly met one of my musical heroes. I had grown up listening to rock 'n' roll and had always admired the work of groups with intricate vocal harmonies. When the Beach Boys burst onto the scene in 1962, I became attracted to their four- and five-part harmonies wedded to electric guitar sounds styled after the work of Chuck Berry. I listened to their top ten hits as they came out on the radio.

When I entered college in 1964 I found that many of my classmates had the LP records of the Beach Boys and I bought many of them for my own collection. When I was in London in 1966 for our semester-abroad program, I heard the Beach Boys LP *Pet Sounds* for the first time and really liked the way the harmonies of the group had been blended with newer, more sophisticated instrumentation and arrangements. At the time I didn't know that this work was really due to the genius of the group's leader, Brian Wilson.

In the years after 1966, the fortunes of the group declined as the tastes of young people shifted away from cars and surfing, but I was still a fan and bought all their LPs and kept close watch over how their new releases were faring on the charts.

In Los Angeles, shortly after my visit to Morning Star Ranch, I used to wander over to a large record store on Fairfax Avenue in Hollywood, not far from my cousin's house where I was staying. In the record store I would look at the music magazines with their charts of the bestselling single releases. That summer the Beach Boys released a single "Do it Again," which tried to recapture their glory days of surf and beach tales and it was a modest success, reaching about number twenty on the charts. I attentively watched its upward progress in my daily visits to the record store.

One day, as I was about enter to the store on Fairfax Avenue, out walked a tall figure with black hair combed to one side, clothed in a white t-shirt and white pants. I instantly recognized who it was, and said, "Brian Wilson!" He turned to me and without hesitation struck up a friendly conversation.

"I was trying to get a light box for my room," Wilson explained.

During that era young people used to place different kinds of lights in a darkened room and watch the effects that they made on luminescent paint on the ceiling and walls. It was a way to either simulate or enhance a psychedelic drug experience.

We started talking and instead of going into the record store, I turned around and walked with Wilson down the street. I was on one side of him. I can't remember if it was the right or the left side. But it was the wrong side.

"Can you move over to the other side? I am deaf in one ear," he said.

I explained to him how I had come across the country from New York, to which he said, "Be sure to visit the beach while you are here."

That might be a natural statement from the founder of the Beach Boys, but it turns out that he never was an avid surfer.

As we were walking, I wanted to know if psychedelic drugs had played any role in his creative process. I had been reading the works of various writers who contended that drugs were a way to enhance the creative process and also to experience mystical states.

"Which helped your music more, acid or grass?" I asked.

"Grass," Wilson answered.

Maybe it was not such a good question, because the sad thing is that not long after this encounter, Wilson broke down completely. He could no longer make music and spent much of the 1970s and 1980s as a recluse, strung out on drugs. His silken voice which had produced amazing falsetto high notes was completely destroyed by cocaine and other drugs.

After a few more steps we reached his car. It was a canary colored Porsche sports car. I was attentive to every detail and noted that through the back windshield I could see a copy of the Moody Blues' mystically inspired record *In Search of the Lost Chord*.

As we got into the car, Wilson looked at me and with all sincerity said, "If you ever get a car, can I recommend a Porsche?"

Wilson drove the car through LA's traffic and I remarked that his latest single had "only" reached number twenty. "Many people would give their eye-teeth to get to number twenty," he rightly replied.

We entered one of the many highways that weave their way through and around the Los Angeles metropolitan area and stopped at a hamburger stand, an Orange Julius fast food restaurant. We ate and spoke some more and then Wilson drove me back to my cousin's house. On the way back I explained how my cousin and his friends had a rock 'n' roll group and were trying to make it in the music business. I explained that the group used to perform in their house before wild parties of young people. When

I described the scene at my cousin's house, Wilson noted that his brother Dennis had stumbled into something similar in the LA area. I didn't know it at the time, but it was a reference to Charlie Manson's commune. Dennis Wilson had befriended Manson, who in addition to being a crazed commune leader, was also an aspiring musician.

As the car drew up to the house on Santa Monica Boulevard, Wilson gave me his personal telephone number and we said goodbye.

Brian Wilson was not the only famous musician I met that summer. One of the members of my cousin's band was Chris Mancini, the son of Henry Mancini, an American composer, conductor and arranger, best remembered for his film and television scores. Henry Mancini was at the height of his success in this period.

One day Henry Mancini entered the house and Chris and one of the other band members treated him to an acoustic blues guitar jam. Henry stayed for a while and then left. A few days later Chris came back to the house and said that when he went home he found that his father had been apparently impressed with their guitar playing and was now fooling around with a guitar.

I almost met another great musician that summer. One day, my cousin said, "Let's go to Laurel Canyon and meet my friend Frank Zappa." Laurel Canyon was a beautiful area where a lot of rock stars had houses with scenic views. Frank Zappa was an avant-garde guitarist who achieved huge success in the 1960s. We reached Frank Zappa's house and my cousin knocked on the door. Out came Frank Zappa's wife and she explained that her husband was not home. She showed us around the place. I remember that there were a number of man-made caves in the back yard, giving it an unusual look much in keeping with Zappa's eccentric image.

During that first visit to California in the summer of 1968, I got a good glimpse into the spiritual possibilities that were then available in the US. While sitting in San Francisco's Golden Gate Park I saw someone doing Tai Chi for the first time and thought it quite strange. I got invited to the Hare Krishna temple and had an Indian dinner for the first time, which also seemed strange, and while eating I listened to a sermon on the Bhagavad Gita.

Back to New York for More Spiritual Seeking

After two months in California, I returned to New York City where I was supposed to enter graduate school. However, I was no longer interested in studying international affairs. I wanted to pursue "internal affairs" and Herman Hesse's *Siddhartha* and similar books held much more allure for me than courses in capitalist economics. I only went to a few classes at Columbia and then dropped out to pursue my real interests.

In New York I continued my spiritual searching. I went to a lecture by Swami Satchidananda in Carnegie Hall. The hall was filled to capacity by "flower children." Swami Satchidananda was an orange-robed Indian yogi with a long white beard. He really looked like a guru. At that time he was enjoying the patronage of the famous artist Peter Max and would later go on to give the opening invocation at the Woodstock Music Festival held in August 1969. I still remember parts of his lecture. For example, he said if you make a list of all the things you are attached to such as "my house," "my car," "my camera," etc., then look at the list; all these things, he said, stand between you and liberation.

Despite my interest in his lecture and the things that he was talking about, I did not go to him or his organization to receive instruction. I was not ready for that.

I continued to explore the spiritual realm, reading many books and even taking courses in astrology. One of the most popular books at that time was Edgar Cayce's book on prophecy. Cayce was a simple man who went into trances in which he was able to diagnose and prescribe cures for people who were not physically near him. In his trances he also foretold of events to come and said that a great spiritual era was about to manifest. This inspired me greatly. I really wanted to be part of this new era but didn't know how to do it.

This is a Beautiful Place!

Nineteen sixty-eight was a year of youth unrest around the world. Students brought Paris to a standstill. There were demonstrations in Mexico, and demonstrations in the US against the war in Vietnam reached a new peak with a violent confrontation between police and demonstrators outside the Democratic National Convention in Chicago in August.

All this turmoil was certainly one of the main reasons that I was now on a quest to find something new. After dropping out of Columbia University, I wandered around New York City hoping to uncover the next steps on my path.

One day I was in Tompkins Square Park in the East Village on New York's Lower East Side. This park was the first place where the founder of the Hare Krishna movement held his outdoor chanting sessions starting in 1966. Today there is a plaque in the park commemorating the event, but on that gray autumn day as I sat on broken park bench there was no plaque, nor was there any chanting or drumming in the air. It was a bleak day in a seedy park.

Then I looked up and saw someone whom I instantly recognized. It was the frizzy-haired Abbie Hoffman. Hoffman was one of the leaders of the demonstrations in Chicago and was indicted in the Chicago Seven Conspiracy Trial in which he and his codefendants sparred with a stern old judge named Julius Hoffman (no relation).

Abbie Hoffman was also one of the founders of the Youth International Party, more popularly known as the Yippies. It was not really a political party but a loose movement of young people who used wild, theatrical means to mock the establishment.

Hoffman was a friendly guy and sat down on the bench with me. He gave me a hardboiled egg and as we ate together, he looked around at Tompkins Square Park and exclaimed emphatically, "This is a beautiful place."

It didn't look beautiful to me. There was dog excrement everywhere and it was as rundown as the neighborhood around it, but Hoffman insisted that it was a great place. He was trying with all the might of his mind to imagine how the park should be and not what it actually was. This kind of idealism fueled his turbulent life.

Hoffman looked at a button that I was wearing. It was a campaign button for someone running for office in Midtown Manhattan. It said, "Jeff Brand Works!"

"Who is Jeff Brand?" Hoffman asked.

I said I didn't really know, because someone had given it to me. Actually I didn't tell him exactly how I had gotten the button.

About a week or two earlier one of my friends paid me a visit and saw that I was wearing a button that simply said Yippie! It was a button distributed by Hoffman's Yippie movement. My friend traded his "Jeff Brand" button for my "Yippie!" button, and when I met Hoffman I was wearing this button and not a Yippie! button.

Who knows how the conversation might have developed if I had had the Yippie button on when I met Hoffman? After we shared the eggs together, Hoffman went on his way. But to my later surprise, Hoffman's view of a beautiful Tompkins Square Park eventually was realized. I visited New York in 1996 after a long period abroad, and my colleague Dada Daneshananda took me for a tour of the city. One of our stops was Tompkins Square Park where we met our friend "Sparrow." Sparrow is a New York humorist and poet whose satiric quest for the Republican Presidential nomination in 1996, chronicled in his book *Republican Like Me*, was definitely in the spirit of Hoffman's Yippie movement. As we walked through the park, I marveled at how it had been transformed. It was summertime and there were lots of families enjoying a warm outing with their children. Everything was clean, the playground equipment was new, and there were no drug peddlers or winos around. It was indeed a very beautiful place. It must be noted that the change in the park was due to the gentrification of the area and not to revolution, but in some way Hoffman's vision was partially fulfilled.

Someone Could Get Killed Here

As 1968 was coming to a close, I was trying to take in everything that the counterculture could offer. I had listened to recordings of a revolutionary rock band from Detroit named the MC5 and was excited to find out that they would soon be playing a gig at the Fillmore East, just a few blocks from where I was living.

Today the MC5 are considered to be precursors of the Punk movement as they had angry lyrics and loud, unsophisticated musicianship, but back then they were known for their radical politics and their association with drugs. Their manager, John Sinclair, was a leader of the White Panther Party, which sought to play a role in the Civil Rights Movement along with the Black Panther Party. Sinclair was later arrested for possessing two marijuana joints and sentenced to ten years in prison. His imprisonment became a cause célèbre that attracted the fervent support of John Lennon and other celebrities.

Back in 1968, the MC5 were already controversial for their obscene lyrics, and their gigs at the Fillmore East were quite eventful due to the intervention of an anarchist group with an obscene name that matched some of the lyrics of the MC5. The anarchist group, whose full name has the acronym UPW/MF, was something like the Yippies, conducting demonstrations to mock the establishment and champion the rights of the downtrodden. On New York's Lower East Side, they opened storefronts serving homeless youth, and when a strike of sanitation workers left mountains of stinking garbage on the streets of their "territory," the UPW/MF activists picked up a lot of it and carted it uptown and dumped it at the Lincoln Center in protest.

After the garbage incident, the UPW/MF found another cause. They objected to the activities of rock impresario and concert promoter Bill Graham, who had turned an old theater on Second Avenue into the Fillmore East. They claimed that Graham was making a lot of money by showcasing the top rock groups of the day, and that he didn't contribute anything to the local community. They forced their way into a performance of the Living Theater that was taking place at the Fillmore and later threatened Graham with death if he didn't open up the theater to the community. As a result Graham reluctantly agreed to hold free concerts on Wednesdays.

I went to one of the free concerts and got to see what happens when an anarchist rock band, an anarchist street group, and an adamant rock promoter get mixed together in an uncomfortable combination. The MC5 were to be the headliners and I went to the concert expecting a good performance. Unfortunately I made the mistake of taking a psychedelic drug before the concert. Most people said that if you want a good experience or a mystical experience with LSD, you should do it in a peaceful environment, and that was why hippies flocked to New York's Cloisters, a museum featuring medieval art and a beautiful, large park on the northern tip of Manhattan.

The night the MC5 played at the Fillmore, it was nothing like the Cloisters. The place was packed and when the group opened their set with their loud guitars, I became paranoid. I thought, Someone could get killed here tonight. At first I believed that it was the drug that was making me frightened or maybe the music, but there was something else going on. The truce between Graham and the anarchists was only temporary.

Midway through the concert, members of the UPW/MF stormed the stage. They proclaimed that the Fillmore was now liberated territory. Bill Graham didn't want to put up with this and he, too, got up on stage and started arguing vehemently with the anarchists. "It's my theater," he said. The situation was getting ugly and then all of a sudden Pete Seeger jumped on stage with an acoustic guitar. He started singing the Cuban song "Guantanamera" and somehow everything became peaceful.

The music was over for that Wednesday night and we filed out of our seats and headed to the entrance on Second Avenue. In the lobby I noticed right in front of me a slender man with a pony tail. It was the Beat poet Gary Snyder. I had recently finished reading his book *Earth House Hold*, a collection of essays which went on to become a pioneering text of the emerging ecology movement. I didn't try to say anything to Snyder. No one was saying much of anything in the lobby. We were all just happy to be leaving in peace.

We got out of the concert without experiencing any real violence, but a few weeks later the MC5 came to the Fillmore again and this time the UPW/MF turned on the group, whom they considered to be sell-outs, and burned some of their equipment right on stage and brawled with Bill Graham's security personnel. My initial premonition was not far from the mark.

Bumping into Ginsberg

While I was living in Manhattan one of my pastimes was visiting bookshops on the Lower East Side. I was mostly looking for books about meditation, psychology, expanding consciousness, the New Age, and related subjects.

On St. Marks Place, the hippie epicenter, and the streets around it, there were a few bookshops where it was okay to browse and read the books too. The shelves of these shops were filled with the latest releases as well as old classics that had been republished to meet the growing demand of a new generation. You could read books by William Blake, Aldous Huxley, Tim Leary, and Hermann Hesse, or pore through The Tibetan Book of the Dead, Tao Te Ching and the I Ching. I felt that these bookshops were the hub of a new culture and thought that these were the places where I had to be if I wanted to discover the secrets to my own inner self and find out where humanity was headed. I spent a lot of time in the bookshops.

There were two stores that stood out. The first was Samuel Weiser, a long-established bookstore that specialized in selling and publishing occult, esoteric, and spiritual books. It was not a hippie establishment like some of the newer bookshops, but as I was at that time avidly interested in astrology and Eastern mysticism and as it was located just a few blocks from St. Marks Place, it also became a place where I visited from time to time.

The other famous bookshop on the Lower East Side was the Peace Eye Bookstore, which in 1968 was on Avenue A facing Tompkins Square Park. The Peace Eye was the brainchild of poet and activist Ed Sanders. Sanders was one of the ringleaders of the counterculture's assault on standard American norms, and both his band, The Fugs, and his bookshop reflected his personality perfectly. The Peace Eye didn't have slick shelving and fixtures like big chain bookshops and looked like it was thrown together with whatever materials were at hand. One day as I was browsing the books at the Peace Eye I noticed a hand-lettered sign, which seemed to have been drawn with a crayon on an old piece of cardboard. It was dangling from the book rack and solemnly warned, "This store is protected by a genital-devouring fruit bat."

Visiting these bookshops must have gotten to me, because in the early months of 1969 I got the bright idea to start my own bookshop. I started looking around for a location that I could afford and found a dilapidated storefront on Avenue C near Tenth Street. My friends used to joke that the western part of the East Village at Third Avenue bordering Greenwich Village was civilized but that when you went further east, crossing First Avenue and then Avenues A, B, C and D, you were "entering Vietnam." Indeed this was a place of drug addiction, poverty, and high crime. Policeman patrolling by foot on Second Avenue used to walk in pairs, fully armed, each with a big dog on a leash. I used to think to myself, "They are armed to the teeth but what about us? How are we to survive in this jungle?"

So Avenue C was not the greatest of locations but it was all that I could come up with. With what limited funds I had I went to Weiser's bookshop which had a wholesale division and bought some books on spirituality. I went to another wholesaler and got other books that I thought would interest my counterculture clientele and got ready to open my bookshop.

I announced that it would open on June 3. Henry Weingarten, an acquaintance who went on to become a well-known astrologer specializing in financial predictions, told me that this date "had a powerful chart." To add to the mystique of the opening, I told my friends that poet Allen Ginsberg was going to come into the shop on opening day. I didn't know Ginsberg personally and didn't know how to invite him, but I had heard that he lived somewhere on Tenth Street and I had once seen him walking in midtown Manhattan. In my mind it was possible that he might drop in.

Sure enough, in early afternoon of June 3, Ginsberg and a friend (who might have been his partner Peter Orlovsky) walked into the shop. He greeted us, browsed around and then walked out. It was not a big encounter, but my friends standing next to me were impressed by my "predictive" abilities.

Things went downhill from there. I did not have enough money to set up a proper bookshop. I didn't have enough books to fill up the shelves and couldn't present them properly. The Peace Eye bookstore looked like a palace compared to mine.

Despite the thin selection of books and the store's hopeless location, I did attract some attention. One afternoon a stocky, middle-aged man dressed in a sport coat came in and started to browse the books. He was looking around, and then it dawned on me that he didn't look like the usual type of person hanging around in the East Village. I think he was an undercover police officer, probably sent to see if this new place was some kind of drug-related site or the headquarters of dangerous radicals.

If he was a police officer on the lookout for nefarious doings, what he saw next might have put him at ease. A young African-American boy came into the store and asked me if I could make change for a five-dollar bill. I went to my "cash box," which was an old cigar box, and opened it. There was not much in it but I managed to make the change, handing the boy some one-dollar bills and some coins. The book browser was looking at me fumble through the small change and then after a short time left the shop.

Though I didn't have expensive fixtures, much inventory or cash, one night someone broke into the store. When I came in the morning the doors were open and some things inside had been tossed around. I was angry and depressed by this event. The euphoria of being in the East Village, searching for spirituality, and getting ready to usher in the Age of Aquarius had evaporated. On top of the store break-in, I had already been held up by knife-wielding drug addicts two times in the weeks before. I was now ready to move to a new location.

Back to California

In August 1969, I closed the bookstore, and got ready to head west again. As I was about to leave I saw posters announcing "Three Days of Peace and Music" at a festival that would be held in upstate New York. This was the announcement for the famous Woodstock Festival. However, I was so anxious to get out of New York that even the allure of the best bands of the day could not keep me from leaving immediately.

I traveled to Los Angeles where I attended my first yoga class. It was conducted by Yogi Bhajan, an Indian Sikh teacher who was just starting out his work in LA. He would go on to become one of the most influential of the New Age gurus in the US. After attending the class I remember walking down a street and all of a sudden I felt a tremendous feeling of well-being that just seemed to descend on me. I felt like I was walking on air.

But still, despite this first experience in a yoga class, I was still restless and not yet ready to go into the practice on a regular basis. Once when I was hitching around Los Angeles, someone suggested that I go up to

Washington State and take part in the apple harvesting there. He said they paid good money and provided a place to live and it was interesting work. I didn't make it to the apple fields but I did go north. After a brief journey to a rock festival in Washington State I ended up in Berkeley, California.

By this time I was tired of traveling. I was not sure what to do next. I had traveled from New York to California twice and up and down the West Coast and was now at a standstill. I had enjoyed the experiences on the road but the restlessness and curiosity that were driving me onward were not satisfied yet. I felt I had to decide on something. I didn't want to go back east, and couldn't go any further west without landing in the ocean. It was a short-lived dilemma, for I was about to take some steps that would shape the rest of my life.

One day in Berkeley I was in a bookstore and saw something that interested me. It was the catalog of the Mid-Peninsula Free University. The Mid-Peninsula Free University was a kind of ad-hoc counterculture institution working in the area near Stanford University, in Palo Alto. The classes were held in people's houses. This area is now known as Silicon Valley, the heart of the software and computer industry in the US.

The courses in the catalog were quite interesting, covering everything from cooperatives to art to gardening. These were topics that held my interest. Then I remembered that one of my college classmates had gone on to do his graduate work in Stanford University. I went to visit him and slept on his living room couch for a few days. He was a resourceful person and helped me to get a job in the Stanford University Library. I then got a room in a house rented by some Stanford University students, and I now had a base in this interesting area.

The work at the library was routine and not my main interest. I continued to read all kinds of spiritual books, picking many of them from the shelves in the library basement. I also signed up for some courses from the

Mid-Peninsula Free University catalog. The first one I took was called "The Art of Giving Away Bread." I learned how to bake bread and give it away.

In October of 1969, the college students I was sharing a house with said they were going to a Halloween party and that at the party there would be some people from New York whom I might enjoy meeting. I went to the party and found out that some of the people to whom I was introduced were visionaries who wanted to start a cooperative movement in the US. The large scope of their plans caught my imagination and the next day I signed up for a course they were offering as part of the Mid-Peninsula Free University. It was not just a theoretical course. They wanted to start a seed cooperative right in the Palo Alto area and then buy some land in Oregon where they could develop and implement their ideas further. Some of the people in this group rented a house in Menlo Park and began pooling their earnings with the goal of buying land in Oregon. They asked me to join and in January 1970 I moved in.

One of the members of this community was Jan Derksen, a young man from Holland who was a research fellow at the Stanford Research Institute. He became my best friend and shared my interest in spirituality. We visited Zen teachers, took a trip down to Los Angeles to attend a special festival at Yogi Bhajan's center, listened to the talks of Steve Gaskin in Golden Gate Park, saw the Hare Krishna guru, Prabhupada, in Golden Gate Park, signed up for Kundalini Yoga courses at Stanford, attended Transcendental Meditation lectures, and did whatever we could to find out more about the spiritual path.

In the summer of 1970, our whole community traveled to Grass Valley, California, and met Swami Kriyananda, who had founded a rural community where he hoped to implement the ideas of his guru, Paramahansa Yogananda. When I was growing up, I used to read the book review section of the *New York Times* and there was always an advertisement with an Indian man with shining eyes staring out from the newspaper pages. That was an advertisement for the book *Autobiography of a Yogi*, the life story of Yogananda. At that time I had no interest in the book, but now I was reading it with great interest. In the book Yogananda described his meeting with an elusive guru named Babaji. I say "elusive" because it was not really clear if he was an actual being who lived and died or a spirit who mysteriously appeared, disappeared, and reappeared before spiritual aspirants.

The book inspired me and it was also good to meet Swami Kriyananda. While reading Yogananda's *Autobiography*, I came upon a passage where he said that even if someone just repeats the name of Babaji he or she would get a spiritual blessing. So I repeated that name a few times and was curious and hopeful about what might come next.

2

The Path of Bliss

MY ADVENTURES IN California and my reading of spiritual books prepared me for the most important event in my life. Sometime in November 1970, there was a big gathering on the Stanford University campus. Baba Ram Dass gave a lecture and he introduced an Indian yogi, Swami Muktananda. Ram Dass (Richard Alpert) is an American who was formerly a Harvard University professor, then a psychedelic explorer, and finally an influential and persuasive yogi. The night I saw him he gave one of his signature lectures, which I believe was later incorporated into his best-selling book *Be Here Now*. Swami Muktananda was an Indian guru who was making his first visit to the US. He could not speak English and his lecture was translated. I am writing more than forty years after the fact, but I remember one thing about the lecture that impressed me, both then and now. He repeated several times during the discourse: "You must meditate, you must meditate."

After that lecture I was convinced that I had to get into meditation and not just dabble in it. I did not connect with Swami Muktananda after the lecture and did not learn meditation from him, but he prepared me for my next step on the spiritual path.

About a week after the Ram Dass–Muktananda lecture, I saw some posters on the Stanford campus with the picture of an Indian yogi that said, "learn meditation...free of charge." That was all I needed to see. I immediately called the telephone number on the poster and said that I wanted to learn meditation. The person answering the call said, "Why don't you attend the lecture first and then you can learn meditation." This seemed reasonable, so I went to the lecture with some friends. A short Indian man dressed in a turban and orange robes stood behind a podium. There were a lot of young people in attendance, and they were not the suit-and-tie people who had been at a previous meditation lecture that I had attended. Rather they were the long-haired young people with whom I could identify. I don't remember anything about the lecture, but it was good enough to convince me that I must learn meditation the very next morning.

The next morning I went to work in the library and requested a short leave to learn meditation. My leave was granted and I headed to a small house located at 365 Grant Avenue in Palo Alto. The living room of that house was packed with people waiting to learn meditation. I approached someone who was in charge of the arrangements and told them that I only had a short leave from work and requested to get some special consideration. They put me at the head of the line and the next thing I knew, I was alone in a room with the Indian yogi.

During my initiation, the monk taught me a mantra, a secret two-syllable Sanskrit phrase, and told me that by concentrating on it my mind would gradually expand until one day I would be able to perceive the Cosmic Consciousness. I went out and sat in the main hall, closed my eyes, and started repeating the mantra in coordination with my breathing as he had taught me. After a few minutes I started to feel an unusual sense of inner calm and inner well-being, as if I had somehow stepped into another dimension that I hadn't even known existed. My God! I thought. This stuff actually works. Cosmic Consciousness here I come!

Prior to this initiation I had tried to meditate following advice from books or casual instructions given by friends and acquaintances, but I could never really get into any of these practices because I was unsure if I was doing the right practice or whether I was doing any of the practices properly. But now I had the feeling that I had learned a practice that I would be able to stick with and master. That feeling proved to be correct. After my initiation, I did not miss a day, practicing two times a day, then three times a day and then even more. This continues to this very day.

A few days after my initiation, I attended a retreat that had been organized for the initiates from the San Francisco Bay area. It was a huge gathering in a state park or some other similar site (I can't remember exactly). I entered the main hall where everyone was seated and listened to incredible singing and chanting and immediately felt that I was really in the right place: the place that I had been restlessly searching for in my travels.

Following the retreat, I began to meditate twice a day and did whatever I could to learn more about the teachings of the Ananda Marga Yoga Society, the official name of the organization in the US at that time. Ananda Marga is a Sanskrit term that means, "The Path of Bliss."

Going Deeper into Meditation

Immediately after initiation, I began meditating twice a day and I also adopted a vegetarian diet. Not only was it a vegetarian diet but it was the special yogic or *sattvic* (pure) vegetarian diet that excluded eating onions, mushrooms, and garlic. I still went to work every day in the Stanford University Library, but every evening when I got home I did my meditation. I was not sure if I was getting very far in the practice but I did it diligently night and day. My friend Jan and several other people in my little community also were initiated into the Ananda Marga meditation practice and we sometimes did meditation together. A few of us would visit the monk who had taught us meditation as often as we could. We also attended the collective meditation sessions held in the Stanford Student Union.

During one of my visits to the monk's residence in Palo Alto, I met a young artist who had just been to India. He told me that Ananda Marga in India was a vast organization with many social projects and "even their own political party." This intrigued me. I was happy to know that I was part of a large movement that could help change society.

While visiting the yoga house I saw for the first time on the meditation altar a photo of Shrii Shrii Anandamurti, the founder of Ananda Marga. A good-looking, clean-shaven man with folded hands, his civil name was Prabhat Rainjan Sarkar but everyone called him "Baba." This created confusion for some of us because we were not sure if he was the same Baba as the famous Babaji in Yogananda's book. Very soon I would learn more about the Baba of Ananda Marga.

One day the monk announced that he would give a special course for those who wanted to assist him by becoming yoga teachers. I signed up, along with a few of my friends. It wasn't really a course. All we had to do was go to the small house where the monk was staying and meditate with him at 5:00 AM for one hour straight. Previous to this, I was barely able to sit for twenty to thirty minutes. On the last day of the course, he then showed us which yoga postures to do and to teach. He also said that now that we were going to be yoga teachers, we should meditate three times a day instead of the customary two times.

Immediately thereafter, whenever I was working at the library, I would divide my lunch hour into two parts. During the first part of the lunch hour I would sit on a bench or on the campus lawn and meditate, and during the second part I would eat my lunch. Before going to work I meditated and immediately upon returning home from work I meditated again.

Once again, I was not sure if I was making much progress in meditation, but I was certainly doing more of it.

Now that I was "qualified" to teach yoga classes, I soon got my chance. Sometime around February of 1971, another retreat was organized. This time it was in a campsite near Santa Cruz. Once again several hundred young men and women from all over Northern California attended. The monk in charge of the retreat organized a midnight meditation on the first night, so we dozed off getting ready for that meditation. While I was resting, someone tapped my shoulder and asked me if I would teach a yoga class the next morning. I said yes and got some more rest before the midnight meditation.

The next morning, the organizers divided the retreat participants into two large groups. I was assigned to one of them in a large open area and taught my first Ananda Marga yoga class to about 150 people.

A Life-Changing Event

After my second retreat I continued meditating regularly, three times a day. Sometime in late February or early March 1971, I heard that the monk was going to conduct a special intensive course. I was not sure what this course would entail but some of the *margis*, as the members of Ananda Marga are called, said that he would teach more lessons in meditation and that I would "get high." This sounded interesting so I got ready to apply for the two-week course. My intention was to take the course and then go back to my friends in the Palo Alto area and continue with the work of building our community and eventually move to Oregon to set up a rural cooperative community.

However, when I went to see Dada (the Ananda Marga monks are addressed as "Dada," which means "respected elder brother") to talk about my application to attend the course, my plans and my life changed. When I entered the room, Dada asked me what I did. I said that I worked in the library at Stanford University. He looked at me and said, "You work in the library?" I had a big beard and long hair and was dressed in blue denim overalls and a t-shirt, very unlike the typical library assistant.

Then he said, "After you complete this course, can I send you anywhere in the US to work for our mission?" I thought about it for only a few seconds before replying yes. That yes was to change the entire course of my life. No longer was I thinking of returning to Palo Alto and my old plans. I was ready to help build Ananda Marga in the US and beyond.

YOU Seminar and Baba Nam Kevalam

Shortly after my interview with Dada, I got ready to attend the YOU seminar. YOU was the acronym for the non-profit organization Youth for an Orderly Universe, which Dada had just set up. I never liked that name because it sounded "goody-goody." I was in a more revolutionary mood at the time, but I went to the seminar to go deeper into meditation.

There were over sixty participants for the two-week program, which took place at a campsite located in mountains outside of LA. We meditated many hours a day—I seem to remember the number of hours being eight, but I could be wrong about that. In addition to the meditation, Dada gave classes on Ananda Marga philosophy and I was able to grasp enough of it to be able to start teaching it as soon as I left the seminar. We did a lot of chanting and singing during our stay. Many of the songs were Hindu chants that have become very popular in the kirtan movement in American yoga circles. We were also introduced to the chant *Baba Nam Kevalam* and an accompanying dance that went along with it. This is the kirtan mantra of Ananda Marga.

Kirtan (or more properly spelled *kiirtan*) means chanting the name of God. It was first popularized in India five hundred years ago by the saint Chaitanya Mahaprabhu. Today in India this kind of chanting is very common in temples, in villages, and in the city streets. We were told that in the last quarter of 1970, Ananda Marga's guru had introduced the mantra *Baba Nam Kevalam* and that its meaning was "only the name of the most beloved." I had heard this mantra a few months earlier at the yoga house in Palo Alto but then it was not a central part of the practice.

The dance that went with the mantra was very simple. We were taught to hold our arms in the air above our heads and alternately tap one toe and then the other behind the heel of the opposite foot in time to the music. Our instructors, who included some Americans who had recently been in India, told us that the chanting would elevate our minds and help us to detach ourselves from the cares of the world and the other thoughts which would disturb meditation. We began dancing in all different directions but they soon had us dance in orderly rows and in the same rhythm. I quickly discovered that the dancing and chanting made it easier for me to concentrate afterward in meditation.

When the seminar came to an end, Dada addressed us all with a list in his hands. On the list was the name of each participant and next to it was the place where each of us was being sent to propagate Ananda Marga.

It was an incredible list. People were designated for places like Alaska, Hawaii, Mississippi, Delaware, just about every state in the Union. What is amazing about this whole thing is that we were all hippies with barely any resources. We got a packet that fit in an 8 ½ by 11-inch envelope consisting of some mimeographed pages about Ananda Marga philosophy and a photo of Dada to be used for posters to advertise lectures and classes. With this packet under our arms and just a few dollars in our pockets, we seminar participants bravely hit the road ready to set up meditation centers all over the country. With our limited means, most of the volunteers had to hitchhike to their appointed destinations.

Finally my name was called and my destination was announced: Santa Monica, California. This was not too far from the campgrounds and seemed to be something manageable. So I, too, left the campgrounds with my backpack, my Ananda Marga information packet, and lots of youthful energy and enthusiasm.

Don't Touch the Swami!

Prior to the training session, Dada had already given a number of lectures in the Los Angeles area and had several contacts there. I was given the name of one young man who would be able to put me up. He lived in the hills above Santa Monica in a small house with a beautiful view. I stayed with him for a few days but then he told me that his mother was coming back so I would have to leave. I wasn't prepared for that but there was nothing I could do. I went out to nearby Venice Beach to see what I could find. I went into a health food shop on the main street and inside I saw a sign that read "Om-Yoga." It looked promising. I copied the address on the poster and found that it was only a few blocks from the health food shop.

It turned out to be on a street that ended where the beach began. It was a beautiful location. I went up to the door of the apartment and knocked, but no one was there. I peered through the windows and then I tried the door and found it open. I looked inside and saw that the main living room was decorated in the style of an ashram: no furniture, a carpet, and something like an altar at one end. It looked peaceful and nice. Although the door was not locked, I thought it best to wait outside on the porch until the owner came back.

Finally someone came. He was a young man who was keenly interested in various spiritual topics. When I explained what I was doing, he said, "I don't really agree with your philosophy but I will give you a place to stay."

He showed me a little alcove and said I could stay there. I rolled out my sleeping bag and was really content with my new home.

Now that I had a secure base, I plunged myself into the work. I found a place in a municipal building located on the Venice boardwalk and was able to set up yoga classes there. Then I took the small photo of Dada and made a poster advertising these classes. After a short time, I learned that a new *acharya* (spiritual teacher) had been posted to take the place of the previous monk. I also found out that he would visit Los Angeles and I began to arrange lectures for his coming visit.

On the day of his arrival, I went to the LA airport with a few friends to meet him. We had difficulty at first finding him but after a time we spotted our orange-robed monk and took him back to the beachfront apartment where I was staying. To my amazement, the apartment was already filled with people interested in meditation. Somehow the word got out that an Indian yogi was coming. In those days, that was all that it took to gather a crowd.

Dada Yatiishvarananda was the new teacher. He was about thirty years old and had previously been an engineer in India. He spoke in an accent that was hard to understand but he had a lot of energy and dynamism. He gave public lectures, which I had organized in the few weeks prior to his arrival, and following the lectures, many people came to learn meditation. In fact, so many people came that it was impossible for him to do anything but teach meditation. He would be seated in one room while I would remain by the door, preparing the people. I explained as much as an assistant could before sending the student into the room to learn his or her particular mantra and meditation method from Dada. He started in the morning and then came out for noon meditation and lunch and went back for another full session in the afternoon.

Dada adjusted pretty quickly to conditions in America but there was still culture clash. During one of the afternoon teaching sessions, he came out of the room, looking shaken. He explained to me that one young woman had just reached out to embrace him. While women hugging and embracing men is nothing new in California, it is a shocking thing for an Indian monk. That's why Dada looked at me and said sternly, "Before sending them into the room tell them, 'Don't touch the swami.'"

Many people learned meditation during these visits and it was very inspiring to be part of it. I remember just before Dada was ready to leave, he embraced me and said, "Think of him with every breath." He was referring to Baba, but frankly up to that time I did not have this kind of relationship with the Ananda Marga guru and that sentence didn't mean much to me.

First Big Retreat, Realizing Baba's Presence

After Dada Yatiishvarananda left Los Angeles, I continued with the work of getting Ananda Marga established. Although the apartment where we welcomed Dada was nice, it was time to move on to something else. While I was working at the Stanford University Library, prior to plunging into this new line of work, I had been earning a regular salary. Part of it I used for my basic monthly expenses and the rest was pooled with the other members of our community into a fund that would later be used to buy land in Oregon. When I left the community, my friends decided to refund the amount that I had contributed over the previous fifteen months. This refund enabled me to work for Ananda Marga and rent a building that would serve as our *jagriti*. Jagriti means "place of awakening" and is the term used for Ananda Marga centers that are home to collective meditation.

Our first jagriti was not a palace. It was an old wooden house on Pacific Avenue in Venice, not far from the beach. Five or six margis moved into the house with me and we had a small spiritual community. This happened sometime in June of 1971.

The next big event looming on the horizon was Ananda Marga's first national retreat, which was going to be held in a church campground near Wichita, Kansas, in July. However, I almost was diverted from attending it. One of the margi brothers living in the house with us had some friends who were in India. They wrote letters to him saying that in India they had met a fourteen-year-old messiah! This fourteen year old, they said, was the "Lord of the Universe."

Well, that was confusing. Although I hadn't really heard much about Baba, I assumed that if anyone was the Lord of the Universe, it would be him and not this fourteen-year- old from India (who later became famous as Maharaji, guru of the Divine Light Mission.)

Just at this time, another person arrived on the scene. He was Bill Bowen or Virupaksa (his spiritual name). He was a British artist married to an American and he had just been in India enjoying the company of Baba. He told us many fascinating stories about his time with Baba, and this helped to keep me on track to attend the retreat in Kansas.

My friend Ken, however, chose to join his friends who had become close disciples of the fourteen-year-old guru, and he soon left Ananda Marga.

He became a disciple of the boy guru who was scheduled to arrive in Los Angeles just as we were leaving for the retreat.

A few days before the retreat, we organized ourselves into cars and got ready to travel from LA to Kansas. We stopped in some campgrounds along the way. One evening I went out to meditate, and then a complaint came from the owner of one of the trailers near where I was meditating. They said, "We don't know what he is doing, but tell him not to do it here."

We finally reached the Assembly of God campgrounds near Wichita, where margis poured in from all parts of the country. It was a retreat filled with devotional songs and Baba Nam Kevalam chanting.

Although the retreat was led by Dada Yatiishvarananda, who had just finished a grueling tour of several American cities where he had taught thousands of people meditation, some of the "stars" of the retreat were the American margis who had recently returned from India. The stories that they told were incredible and fascinating.

An amazing story was told by Pramiil, a tall brother from Wichita, Kansas who became the first president of our association. He was in India during the "*Sadhana* Year," also known as the year of demonstrations, and he attended many *darshans* with Baba. During that special period, Baba illustrated many yoga techniques with demonstrations in which some lucky disciples got to experience higher states of consciousness.

Pramiil participated in one of the demonstrations. Baba said to him, "Pramiil, are you an ordinary little boy or are you an extraordinary little boy?" Pramiil thought about it and knew that whatever he said he would probably be wrong, but to be on the safe side he said, "I'm an ordinary little boy." Baba noted his answer and then told Pramiil to sit on his lap. It is hard to imagine how the tall Pramiil could fit on the lap of Baba, who was only five foot three, but apparently this is what happened.

Baba then called for one of the monks to sit in a meditation posture just in front of him and Pramiil. Baba gave his stick to Pramiil and told him to touch the monk just between the two eyebrows where the nose begins. This spot is sometimes called the third eye or more correctly the *trikuti* (three hills) and is the gateway to the yoga chakra that controls the mind.

When Pramiil touched the monk at the point indicated by Baba, the monk went into a state of deep meditative trance (*samadhi*) and fell backward. Baba then said to Pramiil, "Are you an ordinary little boy, or are you an extraordinary little boy?"

One day during the retreat, Pramiil and the other margis who had seen Baba started telling their stories. Pramiil's narrative was deep and moving, and he concluded by saying, "Baba is always with you."

When he said this, something happened to me. I was seated in a meditation posture and I closed my eyes. Scenes started to race through my head. I saw myself wandering down the main street of Venice worrying about where I would live next. Then I saw myself walking into the health food shop where I saw a yoga poster with an address. Next I saw myself finding that perfect little apartment that was to be the scene of Dada Yatiishvarananda's successful first visit to LA. I saw all of this in my mind and then realized that it was Baba who had arranged it all, that he was showering me with unconditional love and support.

When I realized the kind of love that Baba was giving me, I burst into tears. At this point everybody got up to sing and dance Baba Nam Kevalam, but I could not move from the floor. After a few minutes, I composed myself and got up to join the others in the dance.

From that point on, I realized that Baba was not simply a man who lived in India: he was my guru and his spiritual presence was all around me, guiding me onwards. This was an important milestone on my spiritual journey. From that point onward Dada Yatiishvarananda's advice—think about him with every breath—began to make a lot of sense.

Later I came to know that several other people had experiences like this during that particular session of story-telling, chanting and meditation.

For the first few days of the Kansas retreat, I was in complete bliss. I didn't have a care in the world, but then I remembered a task that the margis in LA had given me. They wanted me to bring back books from the retreat. I began to think about which books I should get and my mind was diverted from the bliss of chanting and dancing. I brought back a good supply of books printed in India and written by Baba, and a new book, *The Path of Bliss*, written by two American disciples who explained Ananda Marga's philosophy in a way that would be understandable to people in the West.

Cleaning Up Our Act

One of the small footnotes to the first nationwide retreat in Kansas was Dada Y's attempt to change the image of his volunteer workers. Most of us came from the hippie movement with long hair, and the men, including me, had beards. Dada Y often said that he didn't like the hippie lifestyle and at the retreat he urged us to cut our hair and get more "trim." One day there was a mass session of hair-cutting and beard trimming. I took part in this and for the next few years, while working as an Ananda Marga volunteer in the US, I was beardless with a mustache and normal length hair.

But Dada couldn't escape all aspects of the hippie subculture. He often told me that he didn't like how the hippies hitchhiked all over California. One day we got ready to go to a lecture that I had organized for him at a college in Santa Monica. The college was a few miles from our house in Venice and we planned to go there by car. We walked to where our car was parked but the driver all of a sudden discovered that he had misplaced the keys. I looked at my watch and saw that we did not have any time to spare. So while the driver rushed back to our house to look for his keys, I quickly grabbed Dada and took him to the main road. I stuck out my thumb and flagged down someone who was driving towards the college.

Dada and I got into the car and the driver was very friendly. He asked what we were doing and I said that we were going to give a lecture on meditation at the college in Santa Monica. He asked who was giving the lecture, and I pointed to Dada, who was sitting sheepishly beside me, frustrated by having had to resort to the hippie mode of transportation.

When we got to the college we found the door to the lecture room locked. I told Dada to wait in front of the room while I searched for someone who could unlock the door. I dashed around the college and it took some time to find the person who could open the door. When I finally arrived back at the lecture room, Dada was not there. I looked out to the college courtyard, and there he was giving his lecture outdoors with a throng of students seated on the grass listening intently.

Work in LA

After the retreat in Kansas, I was really ready to work wholeheartedly for Ananda Marga. I began teaching yoga classes in several localities in the Los Angeles area. I taught yoga postures and introduced the universal mantra Baba Nam Kevalam and some basic meditation. I am not sure how the students felt about the whole thing, but I really enjoyed these classes and experienced a lot of bliss both during and immediately after. In fact, it was this elevating experience that propelled me towards my eventual vocation as a full-time monk and teacher of meditation.

In addition to the yoga and meditation class in Venice, I also taught in Pasadena, Long Beach, and several other places in the sprawling Los Angeles metropolitan area. Some of my students went on to learn meditation from

Dada Y. One of these was Arjuna, a Los Angeles schoolteacher who came to my first classes near the Venice boardwalk. He would later become the pillar of the Ananda Marga community in Los Angeles for many years afterward.

We tried to spread the spiritual message in many ways. One day a few of us heard that there would be a community festival in a Los Angeles park. We went there to see if we could be part of the program. An elevated performance area was set up in the park, and we managed to get on the bill of performers and presenters. We were going to chant some Indian spiritual songs. Just before we were to go on stage, the master of ceremonies asked me, "What is the name of your group?" I thought about it for a few seconds, wildly grabbed the first thought that came to me, and then replied, "The Ananda Marga Sattvic Kirtan Band." He turned around and faced the audience and said, "I can't pronounce their name, but here they are." The audience liked our short performance and we returned home satisfied with a nice outing.

"Liberation of Self and Service to Humanity" is the motto of Ananda Marga. "Liberation of Self" refers to the spiritual side of life, the idea that humans should pursue practices that will bring them union with the Supreme Consciousness (God). The other part of the motto refers to social service. We should render selfless service to society, which is just what the folk-singer Lou Gottlieb had told me a few years earlier. In India Ananda Marga was engaged in widespread social service with hundreds of schools, medical clinics and children's homes. In Los Angeles we did our best to follow this example. Members of our small unit visited a home for children with disabilities and performed music there. The Venice Beach area where our yoga house was located was home to an active alternative and radical community, and I attended meetings that they held to coordinate various activities. I participated in the local food cooperative, which was a large buying club working out of various temporary venues, and joined some coop members in other social activities, including visits to prisoners in local jails. I also taught yoga to people in an alcohol treatment program at the Veterans' Administration Hospital in Los Angeles. A few Ananda Marga members even set up a small daycare center in Venice, trying to fulfill our guru's wish for the founding of spiritual schools around the world. Though our day care center was quite modest, with only a few children, I remember one of the community activists who said, "So many people talked about setting up a daycare center, but Ananda Marga actually did it."

My Life is Really Good

In high school I was a reporter for the school newspaper. I continued this in college as well and also joined the editorial staff in my senior year. I had an aptitude for writing and publishing and when I got into Ananda Marga I applied it to the job at hand. We had a large mailing list because many people had learned meditation from the two monks who had visited Los Angeles. I started to produce a monthly newsletter that contained helpful tips for meditation and excerpts from Baba's writings. It was printed on an old mimeograph machine that a local person made available to us whenever we needed to produce a newsletter.

As the months passed, the newsletter became more sophisticated and started to take the shape of a small monthly magazine. It was still mimeographed but I gave it a grandiose name. I called it "Sadvipra." Sadvipra is the name that Baba gave to the ideal moral and spiritual leaders who he said would emerge in the near future to guide humanity to a bright destiny.

With the yoga classes, social service activities, and newsletter publishing, I was fairly busy and time went by quickly. All of these activities were very fulfilling and one day during 1971, I walked down the boardwalk at Santa Monica beach and watched the sun sinking into the Pacific Ocean. While gazing at the setting sun and at the hills and mountains that joined the ocean at the horizon, I had a feeling that now, at the age of twenty-five, my life was really good. I was almost floating down the boardwalk with the same euphoric steps that I had taken on the streets of LA after my first yoga class.

Where Can I Read More About This Krishna?

On the spiritual path euphoria, doesn't last forever and I still had to face some significant obstacles. One of the biggest problems in my life from 1968 onwards was the draft for military service. When I graduated from college, my student deferment expired immediately. By this time I was fully convinced that the war in Vietnam was immoral and that I didn't want to fight in it. But it was not so easy to get out of it. I was called to two military physicals but was thrown out of them because I disrupted their orderly procedures. If you have ever heard Arlo Guthrie's song "Alice's Restaurant," you'll have an idea of what my first two physicals were like! If you haven't heard the song, then suffice it say when the army encounters a long-haired hippie, things can get strange.

Getting ejected from two physicals delayed the whole process and I went on exploring the spiritual path and getting into Ananda Marga work. In fact, I got so involved with the propagation of Ananda Marga that I more or less forgot about this problem and wasn't even aware of further calls to appear for physicals.

One day, someone knocked on the door of the ramshackle Venice jagriti. It was an FBI officer. I asked him if he would like to come in, but he said no, that we should talk in his car. We got into his car and he said that I was again called for a physical, and I told him that I would go and that there wouldn't be any problem this time.

I went to the physical, and true to my word, I went through all the procedures in an orderly way and was deemed fit to serve in the military. In fact, they were going to administer the oath of induction immediately. But just before they were to begin, the presiding officer said, "Is there anyone here who is going to refuse induction?" I raised my hand and was quickly separated from the rest of the group.

They told me that if I wanted to refuse induction I would have to speak with the commanding officer of the base first. I was taken to a room where an African-American officer was seated. He seemed well educated and intelligent.

He started a discussion and said, "The philosophy of pacifism is not very logical."

I told him that I was not a pacifist but that I didn't think the war in Vietnam was moral. I elaborated by saying, "3500 years ago there was a great spiritual leader named Krishna and he fought in a moral war, but yours is not a moral war so I won't fight in it."

He listened to me intently and then told me that I was free to leave. As I walked out of the door he asked, "Where can I read more about this Krishna?"

After that I never heard from the military, the FBI, or anyone else about these matters. I just went on doing my work with Ananda Marga. Over the years I attributed this to Baba's grace. I was doing his work and he had somehow helped me to continue doing it. Many years later I recounted this story to an old college friend and he listened and then said, "The explanation is easy. The officer was impressed with you and just shuffled your papers to the bottom of the pile." Whatever the reason, a huge problem had been lifted from my shoulders.

The First Jagriti in Beverly Hills

Not long after we moved into the rented house in Venice Beach and proclaimed it an Ananda Marga jagriti, I received a visit from a margi from Philadelphia. He seemed to have a lot of experience in Ananda Marga and when he saw the jagriti he said "Yeah, it's a hole in the wall, just like the others."

His description of the Venice house was not far off the mark. It was an old wooden clapboard building that had certainly seen better days. I didn't think it was that bad, but I was curious to know about the second part of his statement. I hadn't seen other Ananda Marga centers except for the small rented house in Palo Alto and I wanted to know why they had to be "holes in the wall." He explained that we didn't get donations of big houses with swimming pools and other amenities as some religious and spiritual organizations did. "It's just not our style," he said.

I understood what he was trying to stay but I still aspired to one day get something better than the house in Venice. After some time, we had to move out of the house because the landlady was not happy having a spiritual community living on her property. She told us that we would have to find another place.

In the meanwhile I continued teaching yoga around Los Angeles. Joining me during those first months was Naciketa (Steve Richheimer). Steve was a graduate student at Stanford University and was among the first Americans to take initiation into Ananda Marga. He went to India and met Baba and even received his spiritual name from Baba directly. Now he wanted to take some time off to help spread Ananda Marga so he joined me at the Venice jagriti and stayed for several months.

In Venice, Steve and I gave yoga and meditation classes at the municipal building on the boardwalk. When we taught the classes, we wore special clothing, loose white Indian pajama pants called "yogi pants" and a matching Indian kurta. After we finished the first class at the municipal center and got ready to walk out on the boardwalk, Steve asked me "Is it all right to go out on the boardwalk dressed like this or should we change back into our regular clothes?" "Believe me," I said, "it doesn't matter what you wear. Nobody will blink an eye here." Indeed, the boardwalk was well known for all manner of eccentric behavior and still is. In the 1950s, it was a home to the Beat poets and in the late 1960s it became a hippie hangout. Two yogis walking down the boardwalk garbed in Indian clothes in 1971 blended right in with the scenery.

We also taught yoga together at the East-West Cultural Center in downtown Los Angeles. One evening a woman and her husband joined the class. When they came back the next week, the woman was effusive with her praise. "My husband was able to sleep soundly for the first time in years," she said. She went on and on about how good the class was and then finally she said, "We have a house that was damaged in the earthquake; if you two can fix it up, then you can use this as your yoga center."

A few months earlier a strong earthquake, centered in Los Angeles' San Fernando Valley, had shaken the region and many homes had been damaged. I have never been handy with tools and didn't think I would be up to the job of fixing the house. In addition I found the couple, particularly the woman, somewhat strange so I didn't want to take part in the project. Steve, however, was very good with this kind of work and his ears perked up when the woman told him that the house was in Beverly Hills.

It was not actually in Beverly Hills, where tourists come on a daily basis to visit the mansions of movie stars. Rather it was in a hilly area just north of the Beverly Hills municipality. The homes there were upper-middle-class, split-level dwellings, not much different from the homes in suburbs all around the country. But the postal address of Beverly Hills, California, gave it a certain mystique. So we finally accepted the offer and moved into the "Beverly Hills" house. When I gave the news to our headquarters in Wichita, one of the young volunteers congratulated us on this feat.

Steve and I then began the work of fixing the house. The earthquake had left large cracks in the living room walls and in a few other rooms. We plastered the cracks and repainted the walls and in a few weeks the house was looking pretty good. It was at this point that the woman appeared at the house one evening and said, "My husband doesn't agree with this arrangement. You will have to leave, immediately."

My initial misgivings about the deal were confirmed but we did not have much time to think about it. We called up a margi friend, Webster Phillips, who worked in the movie industry as a makeup artist. He promptly pointed out the obvious: "You got the place looking pretty good," he said, "and now she wants to throw you out!" Webster owned a trailer in the San Fernando Valley and told us that we could stay there until we found something more suitable. So we threw our things together and moved from the heights of prestigious Beverly Hills to the down-to-earth Valley, where we stayed in Webster's tiny trailer. Eventually we found a modest apartment not far from the ocean in Santa Monica that became our new Ananda Marga jagriti.

More Retreats and More Practices

While working in Los Angeles and later in other places in the US, my life was punctuated by large retreats every six months, one in midsummer and one during the last week of the year. These retreats were held in the center of the US, usually in Kansas.

At the retreat held at the end of 1971, I was introduced to some new practices. We learned that Baba had revived *tandava*, a dance that dates back to the time of Shiva (5000 BC). In ancient times, it was practiced by warriors because the dance is invigorating and increases courage. The dancers hold a knife in their right hand and a skull or snake in their left hand. The knife symbolizes life and the snake or skull symbolizes death. The dance is a celebration of the victory of life over death.

Tandava was demonstrated at the retreat by margis who had learned it in India. After watching the demonstration, we gave it a go. First we had to jump up once, hitting buttocks with our heels and then landing on our toes while keeping our arms extended horizontally. We jumped again and then we began bouncing on one foot and then the other while lifting the other leg in the air above our waists. I soon got the hang of it and really enjoyed it. Some of the margis from Los Angeles who had accompanied me to the retreat said that I did it well.

At this retreat we were also introduced to a set of practices known as the Sixteen Points. It included dietary guidelines, fasting, moral precepts, and meditation. The Ananda Marga path had become more rigorous, but I was up for the challenge and began to learn and follow the new instructions.

Love is all There Is

In the summer of 1972, we again held our nationwide retreat in Kansas. This time it was at the fairgrounds in the city of Hutchinson. Once again several hundred people attended. They came from all over the US and also from Canada, and we enjoyed a busy program of chanting, meditation and lectures on yogic philosophy.

Our retreat coincided with the Independence Day celebration and the city of Hutchinson invited us to send people to march in the Fourth of July parade. I was busy and decided not to attend the parade. Dada Y and a large delegation of margis headed to the place where the parade was to begin. Some of them traveled in a converted school bus that was painted white with red lettering proclaiming "Ananda Marga Yoga Society of California" on both sides.

When the delegation got back from the parade I asked Dada how it went. He said that when he looked at the people lining the parade route and then looked at his margis, who despite his exhortations still looked like California hippies, he began wondering how he was going to explain this to the Midwesterners. And then it flashed in his mind: Baba Nam Kevalam — Love is all there is.

The bus might have looked strange. The margis didn't look anything like the other people attending the parade, and the mantra they were singing was certainly foreign, but "Love is All There Is" was something that everyone could understand. The margis started singing "Baba Nam Kevalam, Love is all there is," and the crowd applauded. This loose translation of Baba Nam Kevalam had sticking power and even today if you ask most margis what this mantra means, they will simply say, "Love is all there is."

Leaving Los Angeles

In August of 1972, my life was about to change. Dada Y came to Los Angeles again and this time he invited me to join the national office of Ananda

Marga in Wichita. He knew that I was skilled at producing newsletters and that I also had some knowledge of newspaper production from my college days so he invited me to come to Wichita to publish a newspaper for Ananda Marga.

In India, Ananda Marga published newspapers and magazines in several Indian languages. This was a program that Baba considered extremely important. So it was easy to understand why Dada wanted me to leave Los Angeles and start work on the newspaper.

The margis of Los Angeles took me to the bus station and I felt satisfied with the work that we had done in LA. I got on the bus and headed towards Kansas, ready to face a new challenge. After three eventful years in California I was leaving and was not to return there for many, many years.

3

Sadvipra

AFTER ARRIVING IN Wichita, Kansas, I was uncertain about what was going to happen next. I was now in the headquarters of Ananda Marga in the US, and it was a living situation unlike any I had previously been in. Our building was a two-story suburban home with trees out in front and a park-like cemetery in the back. This typical American home looked ordinary on the outside but inside it had been transformed into an ashram and workplace. I lived in a former attic area. We didn't have much furniture so we slept in sleeping bags on the carpeted floor but I really liked living in the attic because I could gaze out at treetops from all sides of the building through the gable windows.

Our Wichita office staff. I am standing just to the right of the word "Marga"

What used to be a garage was now an office with several desks. I was given one desk, a filing cabinet, and a typewriter, and with this equipment I was going to produce a national newspaper for this new organization.

On one of my first days in Wichita, we were sitting around the kitchen table and Dada Y introduced me to some of the people there who had not yet met me.

"Previously Vishvarup (my Sanskrit name at that time) was living in LA, using his savings to support himself," Dada explained to everyone at the table. "Now his savings have been exhausted and he is living on Baba Nam Kevalam."

While I was in Wichita my expenses were paid by Ananda Marga, but when I went on to other assignments, both in the US and abroad, I had to fend for myself, and many times over the next forty years I felt I was getting by only with the grace of an unseen hand—or as Dada put it, through the strength of the mantra of love, Baba Nam Kevalam.

Wichita Social Service

There were a number of young volunteers in our Wichita office. A few of them managed the office, maintaining correspondence with a movement that now had branches around the country. I was there to work on the newspaper, and we also had a young printer and an accountant who were going to launch a commercial print shop. Several margis also joined us who wanted to concentrate on social service activities, working under the banner of Ananda Marga's Education, Relief and Welfare Section (ERAWS). My colleagues who specialized in social service organized a number of activities. They visited homes for children with disabilities, visited prisons, and signed up as assistants with the Red Cross. In the event of an emergency, they would join well-equipped Red Cross disaster relief teams. I took part in some of these activities, playing music for children and was also on standby in case of a natural calamity.

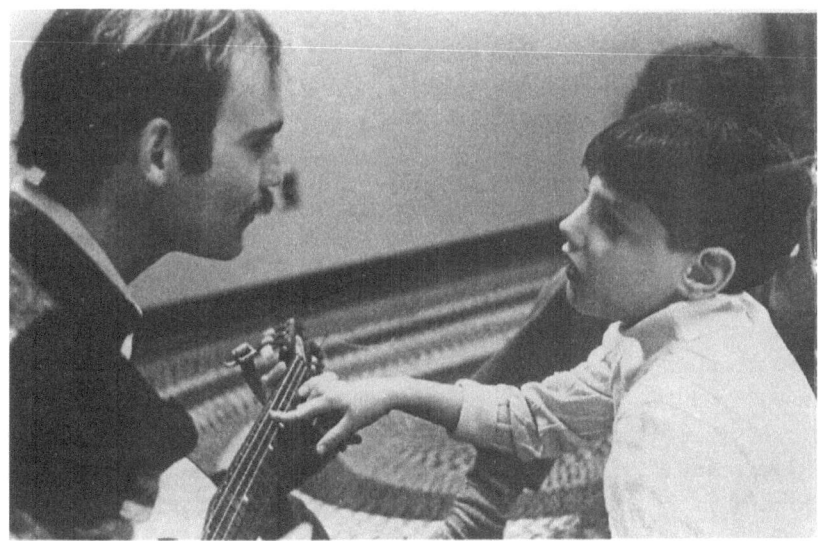

I played guitar and sang at outings to homes for children with disabilities.

We had a great sense of camaraderie. We sang and meditated together every day. We took part in social service activities as a group, and we even played sports together. At one point we decided that one of the best ways to keep in shape and do our sporting activities was to sign up as members of a local gym.

One night a few of us went to the gym to play basketball. There were several middle-aged men on the court when we arrived, so we challenged them to a full-court game. The men were better players than we were, but we had youthful energy and lots of crazy enthusiasm on our side. We ran up and down the court and the older men had difficulty keeping up with us. The game had been going on for a while when someone from our office came and said that the Red Cross had called us. A nearby river had flooded and they wanted us to join their disaster relief team. "Sorry, we have to go now," we told the panting, sweating middle-aged men. As we were leaving I saw one of them lying on his back, letting his breathing come back to normal. I am pretty sure they were very happy to see us leave.

When we returned to our office, we got another call from the Red Cross and they said that the flood was not as bad as they had feared and that we need not come to the disaster scene.

Sadvipra: The Journal of Social and Spiritual Progress

During my first few weeks in Wichita I collected material for the newspaper but I was kind of stalling until I got a wakeup call. Ananda Marga had become very controversial in India at this time. The organization first started out as a small regional yoga movement in the state of Bihar in eastern India. In the early 1960s, Baba created an order of monks and nuns, and they spread the spiritual teachings to the far-flung corners of India. They also set up schools, clinics, and other social service units. Spirituality combined with social service was a good combination and it proved popular. However, Baba also formulated a theory of social change known as the Progressive Utilization Theory, better known by its acronym Prout. Prout challenged both capitalism and communism. I first heard about Prout when the artist in the yoga house in Palo Alto referred to a political party, and later on I started to read Baba's books dealing with social issues. I was deeply inspired by Prout, but in India Ananda Marga was acquiring powerful enemies, especially among the communists who saw Prout as a rival and a threat to their drive to win the allegiance of young people looking for an alternative to capitalism. The left-leaning central government of India became wary of Ananda Marga, as did the Communist-run state government of West Bengal. To combat the rise of Ananda Marga, the government concocted false cases against Baba and on the last day of December 1971 Baba was arrested.

When I heard that Baba had been arrested I was not happy, but I was not overly worried either. We knew about political prisoners in the US. In New York and California, one commonly saw placards calling on the government to free various civil rights leaders, American Indian activists, and many others. Very soon we would be adding "Free Baba" posters to the spectrum of human rights protests in the US and abroad.

The justice system moves a lot more slowly in India than in other parts of the world and it was only in September 1972 that Baba's trial had begun in earnest. Newspaper coverage in India was widespread. When I saw all the Indian newspapers and even a few international articles about Baba's trial, I knew that it was time to swing into action to present our side of the story.

I gathered all my articles together and produced the first issue of *Sadvipra: The Journal of Social and Spiritual Progress*. It was a twelve-page tabloid newspaper. The lead article was about the start of Baba's trial and included a picture of him. There were also essays and articles on spirituality, book reviews, vegetarian recipes, interviews, spiritual comic strips, and other feature articles. Over the next few years, this monthly newspaper became relatively popular and it paid for itself in subscriptions and advertisements. I used to send copies of the newspaper to India to Baba and he read it and even made comments about it.

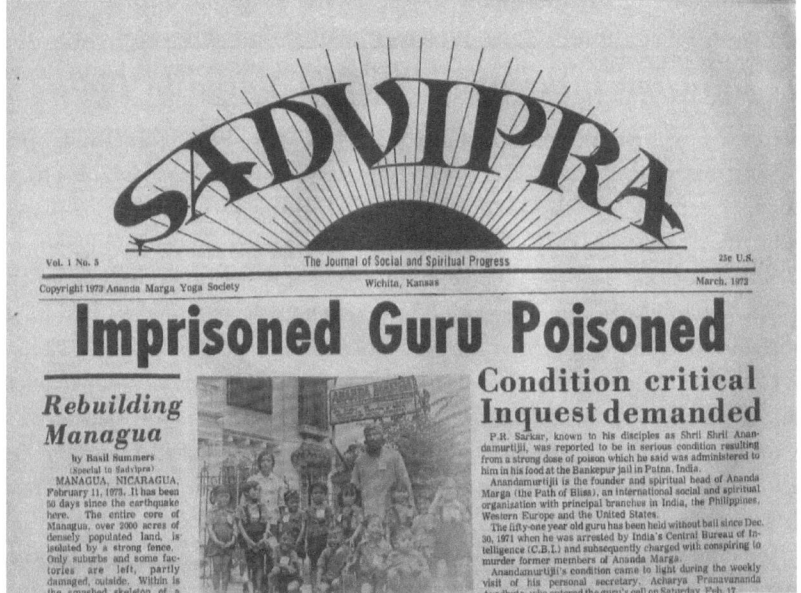

One time he was reading the newspaper and he came upon one of our advertisements. A woman in California was sewing and selling special yogic underwear for men, known as *lungotas*. She advertised it for the price of $2.50 per unit. Baba looked at the price and said, "$2.50! What, are they made out of gold?" (In India at that time the price of a *lungota* would have been 5–10 times cheaper).

Another time, I delayed putting out a monthly issue and combined two issues into one. Someone came back from India and told me that Baba had said, "*Sadvipra* must come out on the same day each month."

Editing and publishing the newspaper was tedious work and kept me very busy. In those days our procedure was as follows: We would type the articles (I would sometimes have one or two assistants), and then bring them to a newspaper plant where they had a typesetting machine. When the typesetting work was done, we would get the articles back in the form of long strips containing columns of type that we would then cut and lay out, attaching the columns by smearing melted wax on the back of the strips and affixing them to a layout grid. We had to cut and paste everything. This was before the era of desktop publishing on the computer, and it sometimes got confusing and messy.

We did most of the work in our own office but on the last day, when the newspaper was to be delivered to the printer for offset printing, we went into the newspaper plant to put on the headlines and do the final layout of the columns of type, photos, drawings, and advertisements. This last day was always the most tedious because of the complexity involved trying to get everything to fit.

Once I was in the newspaper plant and I was taking too much time getting everything ready. The plant owner was annoyed and wanted to go home. He came into the area where I was working and said that he would help me by sending one of his workers to assist me. I was laying out an article that described the yogic chakras, the energy centers situated in the spine. There was a label for each of the seven chakras and they had to be positioned by hand in the right place. Somehow the newspaper assistant got involved in this process and when we got the printed newspaper back, all the labels were in the wrong positions. I and one assistant had to fix it by gluing a correctly labeled chakra diagram on five thousand newspapers. My assistant looked at me and said, "Is this the way it is going to be with every issue?" "No," I said, very sternly.

We continued to publish the newspaper every month, shifting our office from the garage in the yoga house to a room in a commercial print shop that Ananda Marga had set up in Wichita.

Each month we printed close to five thousand newspapers. Some would be sent to individual subscribers and some were sent in bundles to the various Ananda Marga centers in the US. The subscription price was three dollars for twelve issues and somehow checks were arriving in the mail every day. I was able to pay for the cost of printing and mailing the paper from the subscription payments, payments for bulk copies, advertisements, and occasional donations.

"I'm for Evolution!"

Shortly after the first issue of *Sadvipra* was published, I heard that the margis of Lawrence were organizing a lecture for Ram Dass at the University of Kansas. I traveled to Lawrence because I knew that it would be a good opportunity to write an article about Ram Dass and perhaps get a chance to interview him. Baba's trial in India was weighing on my mind and I wanted to find out if Ram Dass, who was by this time quite a celebrity, could help us in any way.

The margis in Lawrence were university students and their apartment was the center for Ananda Marga activities. They hosted a weekly collective meditation session and from time to time they organized lectures on the university campus for Ananda Marga speakers, and in this case, for Ram Dass.

I reached their apartment shortly before the lecture was to begin and after a short time I had a chance to speak with Ram Dass privately. He was seated on the floor in a small room, and he had a confident, self-assured presence. I sat down facing him and introduced myself. After a short time I started talking about Baba's imprisonment.

"It's important for spiritual people to speak up and not allow Baba to be persecuted in this way," I said.

Ram Dass looked at me intently and replied, "As I understand it, in India Ananda Marga stands somewhere between revolution and evolution, and I'm for evolution!"

I got the message. Ram Dass was not about to get involved in this matter so I went on talking about other things. That night Ram Dass gave an inspiring lecture with chanting, similar to the one in Palo Alto that had been instrumental in preparing me for my first meeting with an Ananda Marga teacher. I went back to Wichita and wrote an article about the lecture.

Although Ram Dass did not speak out publicly on behalf of Baba, one of his subsequent books had a section in which the main spiritual movements in America were described and in that section there was a positive entry for Ananda Marga. Also some years later, in Washington, DC, I attended one of Ram Dass's public lectures, and at the end of the lecture I gave him a copy of our newspaper. He took it and gave me a warm smile.

Meeting Mrs. Gandhi in Ottawa, Canada

During the spring of 1973, I found out that India's Prime Minister, Indira Gandhi, was going to pay a special visit to Ottawa . As Baba was still being held prisoner in an Indian jail, several margis wanted to go to Ottawa to let Mrs. Gandhi know how we felt about Baba's imprisonment.

I also learned that it was possible to get press credentials and enter the corps of reporters and broadcasters who would be covering the visit of India's Prime Minister. Using the letterhead of the *Sadvipra* newspaper, I applied and was accepted into the team of accredited print and broadcast journalists.

Margis from different parts of the US and Canada went to Ottawa, planning to hold public demonstrations that would draw attention to Baba's imprisonment. I took a bus from Wichita to Detroit and then to Ottawa. When I arrived in Ottawa, I went to the press headquarters for the Prime Minister's visit and was given complete information about the two-day program. An important piece of information was the places where the Prime Minister would visit during her stay in Ottawa.

With this information the margis were able to organize demonstrations whenever Mrs. Gandhi appeared in public. Margis held "Free Baba" signs and the usual kinds of placards displayed in such demonstrations. But what added zest to the whole thing was the street theater. One margi sister wore an Indian sari and her hair had the characteristic gray-silver streak that Mrs. Gandhi was known for. The street theater showed Mrs. Gandhi presiding over a regime where protesters were beaten and thrown into jail. This was no exaggeration because within the next two years ,Mrs. Gandhi declared a state of emergency in India, suspended democratic liberties and imprisoned thousands of dissenters on all sides of the political spectrum.

The organizers of Mrs. Gandhi's visit were surprised at the quantity of demonstrations because many of her outings in the Canadian capital had not been announced to the public. Everywhere she went, the margis were there. For me the highlight of the event was a press conference in which Mrs. Gandhi took questions from the journalists. As an accredited journalist I attended the conference. When the question and answer session came, I knew I would have a chance to ask her about Baba and Ananda Marga.

Just prior to the press conference we came to know that the persecution of Ananda Marga in India had intensified, and even some Ananda Marga relief projects in a drought-stricken area of India had been shut down by the government. With this on my mind, I carefully framed a question and raised my hand.

As my raised hand was acknowledged and I rose to speak, I was reminded of a similar incident during my last year of college when a representative of the US State Department came to my campus to explain why the US was waging war in Vietnam. I took part in a small meeting with this State Department official and when the question and answer period began, I asked him whether this war was necessary for the defense of the US or if was it being waged for the benefit of vested interest groups. My question was sharply worded and delivered with a lot of zest, and afterward one of my professors came up to me to express his surprise at my frank remarks. This time it was not a small room with a State Department official but a large conference room with Mrs. Gandhi at the podium. I asked her why Ananda Marga social service projects had been closed and why P.R. Sarkar was being held as a political prisoner. She replied that P.R. Sarkar was not a political prisoner but was charged with serious crimes.

When the press conference ended, one of the journalists, who by now had realized that I was not an actual journalist, came up to me and said, "Are you satisfied now?" "Yes," I replied. Without a doubt, the long bus journey and the hectic two days in Ottawa had been well worth it.

I Move to Washington, DC

In September 1973 several people suggested that I would have a better opportunity to develop the newspaper by moving the office to Washington, DC. In Washington a large house had just been donated to Ananda Marga, so I would have a place to stay and work.

At the same time that I moved to Washington, several other margis made the move. They set up a training center in the same house where I would be editing the newspaper. This was to be a training center for the Education, Relief and Welfare Section (ERAWS) of Ananda Marga, where young volunteers would learn Ananda Marga spiritual practices and get a chance to perfect their meditation practice while also working in the field of social service.

The training center was in the upper part of the house and my newspaper office was in the basement. Ten to fifteen trainees were living upstairs, young men and women from all over the US. They did a lot of meditation and chanting, creating a wonderful spiritual atmosphere. During this time, I began to play kirtan and other spiritual songs more and more, and my guitar playing, which I had begun in 1966, was improving.

Some months later, in the early part of 1974, I moved from the training center to a shared house in another part of Washington. My newspaper office moved with me and a Ping-Pong

Prakash Laufer and I (above)

table in the basement of this house became my layout table. 1974 was a year of considerable growth for the *Sadvipra* newspaper. I participated in cooperative mailings with the *East West Journal*, a large New England-based alternative periodical, and our subscriber base increased substantially, going beyond the confines of Ananda Marga. The newspaper continued to feature articles on meditation and yoga, with one of Baba's articles appearing in each issue. There were also articles on martial arts, popular culture, and book reviews that seemed to appeal to our new readership.

After a few months in the shared house, I found an even better place for the newspaper office. A progressive church rented me an office in the Adams Morgan neighborhood. Adams Morgan was the "alternative" section of Washington, DC. When you think of Washington, you might think of the White House and the Capitol building, but not far from these iconic buildings lay a poor neighborhood populated by minorities and young radicals. Food cooperatives and activist organizations made their home here, and so did the *Sadvipra* newspaper in a one-room office.

When we were in Wichita, we used to print the newspaper in a local newspaper plant that published several weekly newspapers, most notably an Air Force base newspaper. In Washington, DC, we found a newspaper plant in Maryland that primarily printed the *Carroll County Times*. It was a long drive from Washington but they gave us the lowest price.

Our routine was much the same as in Wichita. We would do a lot of the work in our own office, but on the day when we brought everything to the printer for submission there was still a lot to be done, such as adding the headlines, getting the photos and illustrations processed and submitting last-minute articles that were typeset right there at the plant and then hurriedly inserted into the layout. We would sometimes spend as much as twelve hours at the newspaper plant. After we submitted everything, we waited and watched as the paper rolled off the huge presses. It looked almost miraculous as the large press rolled out the paper, printed the pages on both sides and then cut and folded the newspaper into neat bundles. Then we stuffed the papers in our van or car and drove back to Washington in the wee hours of the morning.

One night at the *Carroll County Times* stands out in my memory. I was working with the printer trying to get the photographs just right. They used to process the photographs by putting them under a special reproduction camera and producing a grayscale negative (with the dot pattern that you see if you look closely at printed images in newspapers). These negatives were then "stripped" into the layout, and the whole thing was again photographed and made into a plate.

It was after midnight and we were working with such intense concentration trying to finish everything that we didn't notice everyone else leaving the newspaper plant. Eventually we found out that there had been a bomb threat made to the owners of the printing plant. It seemed that a mob or criminal elements had been trying to coerce the plant owners into dropping the newspaper of one of their rivals. I didn't care about any bomb. I just wanted to finish the newspaper and I wouldn't let the printer quit either. At one point he just looked at me and said, "I don't even know why I am doing this for you." Being the devotee that I was, I just thought, he is doing it because it is for Baba's mission.

Later we shifted our printing to a newspaper plant in Silver Springs, a suburb adjacent to Washington, DC. It was closer to our office and made things easier.

Universal Times and Proutist Forum of America

I had started the *Sadvipra* newspaper at the request of Dada Y, who I believe was trying to replicate the kind of activity that Ananda Marga was doing in India but there were some differences between our paper and those in India. In the US, it was not really economical or practical to print a newspaper on our own presses. To produce a tabloid newspaper, you needed a printing press that costs hundreds of thousands of dollars, while the Indian Ananda Marga papers were often printed on our own presses located in our offices.

Another difference between what I was doing and the work that was going on in India is that many of the newspapers that the margis published there were not newspapers focused on spiritual matters but rather analyzed the news from the perspective of Prout (the Progressive Utilization Theory).

I actually wanted to do something similar in the US. I was keenly interested in Prout right from the beginning. Just before I got into Ananda Marga, I was propelled by two forces. I was attracted to spirituality but I was also dissatisfied with the war and other social problems and was looking for progressive social change. I reached Ananda Marga first because of my desire to learn meditation, but I was happy to know that the guru also had something to say about society and that his social message was in line with my bent of mind.

Now I really wanted to spread Prout's concepts of economic democracy and social justice far and wide. I wanted to produce a newspaper that would be based on a Proutist perspective of the world so I decided to alter the course of the newspaper. We changed the name to *The Universal Times* and I even started a separate organization, The Proutist Forum of America, which I registered as a tax-exempt non-profit organization. We chose that name to emulate the Proutist Forum of India.

Though we continued to publish spiritual and cultural articles, *The Universal Times* concentrated more on social issues. Living in Washington, I was able to meet and get contributions from some notable people. At that time Colman McCarthy was a columnist for *The Washington Post*. He was an interesting person who had started his career as a Trappist monk before becoming a peace activist, a journalist, and later a university professor. He was a deeply spiritual person with a strong social conscience and his columns at *The Washington Post* were not like the usual newspaper opinion-editorial essays.

I met him because he was a member of the church that owned the building where my newspaper office was located. Shortly after we met, he began contributing articles to *The Universal Times* every few months. During the time I was in Washington, publishing *Sadvipra* and *The Universal Times*, we also published an exclusive interview with Black Panther leader Huey Newton, who told of his experiences with meditation while being held in solitary confinement.

I also went to a meeting with the late economist John Kenneth Galbraith and wrote an article about him. My attendance at a press conference with consumer advocate and activist Ralph Nader allowed me to write an article that we put on the front page of our paper along with Nader's photo. Someone told me that when they gave the newspaper to Nader, he was beaming.

In addition to meeting the columnist Colman McCarthy, my work on *The Universal Times* allowed me to meet other notable journalists. During this period, I attended a journalist's convention in New York City organized by a short-lived trade publication. One of the main speakers was the newsman Mike Wallace. He was known for his no-nonsense interviews of public figures on his weekly television broadcast. After his presentation, I ran into him in the lobby and began to tell him about Baba. When I told that Baba had been fasting for three years in protest against a poisoning attempt on his life while in prison, he said, "Three years? Jesus Christ!"

Making a Living

When I was in Wichita, Dada Y had said that now I was living on Baba Nam Kevalam. That was only partly correct because when I moved to Washington, DC, I needed to raise a small amount of money each month for my personal expenses. By that time I had become a fairly good typist, churning out articles for the various Ananda Marga newsletters and the *Sadvipra* newspaper. Back in high school I had also taken a course in touch-typing, so that course combined with a lot of practice turned me into a "professional" typist.

Well, I was not quite professional yet, but I went to a temporary work agency in Washington, DC, and was given a typing test. I barely passed, but the firm took me on anyway and they soon gave me temporary assignments in various commercial offices in the Washington area. I would work a few days a week, enough for me to get by. The expenses of the newspaper were paid via a steady stream of subscriptions and payments for bulk orders from Ananda Marga centers around the country.

In addition to temporary office work, I also was able to earn some money on spot jobs that some of my fellow margis organized. One of our brothers was working with a theater company in Washington, and one day he came to the jagriti and said that the company was looking for some caterers to supply some meals for the cast of a musical. I and a few other margis volunteered to take the job.

That first weekend we prepared an elaborate vegetarian meal for the cast. They said that they liked it but some of them insisted on having meat. The next weekend we prepared a chicken dinner but it just did not feel right to be handling the parts of a dead animal in order to make a living. We resigned from the job after that weekend.

More interesting than the catering job was the valet parking business that one enterprising margi, Bruce, started. He organized small groups of young men to park the cars of celebrities and politicians at fancy Washington parties and sometimes invited residents of the jagriti to take part. The parties were held in private homes and mansions in the Northern Virginia suburbs adjacent to Washington, DC. I had heard that our valet parking crew had worked a party for Senator Ted Kennedy one weekend and I was hoping to get a glimpse of something similar.

I soon got my chance. One night I parked cars for guests at a party at the home of Lady Bird Johnson and her family. Mrs. Johnson was the wife of the late President Lyndon B. Johnson and lived near Washington with her daughter Lynda and her son-in-law, Charles Robb, who eventually became the Lt. Governor of Virginia as well as a two-term US senator. Though we parked many cars for guests that night, some of whom must have been well-known public figures, I did not recognize anyone. However, at the end of the party Mrs. Johnson invited the parking team into the house and gave us some refreshments. She personally shook the hand of each of us. As she was shaking the hand of my friend Ram Kumar, I felt that it was very ironic. Ram was the head of our Prout department and she was a symbol of the Establishment. If she only knew with whom she is shaking hands, I thought. But for her, Ram was just a nice young man who had contributed to the success of the party, and the handshake was a pleasant end to the evening.

Bruce didn't stop with valet parking at parties. He soon landed the parking concession at the Pisces Club, a popular downtown Washington destination for the area's rich and famous. I was told that singer and social activist Eartha Kitt sometimes visited the club, as did various politicians.

One night I was on duty in the parking lot of the Pisces Club when a giant American sedan, of the type that was popular before gasoline prices started to rise in the 1970s, roared into the parking lot. The parking lot was not exactly level. There was an incline and then a dip at the entrance to the lot. The sedan that came in was going too fast and the underside of the car scraped against the bump, causing sparks to fly. It was not a serious problem, but I was surprised when the car door opened and out stepped Senator John Glenn, the first American to orbit the earth and a huge public hero. I looked at him and he looked at me with the glance said, "Yeah, I know that you recognize me." He smiled and I parked his car.

That was another ironic meeting. The man who orbited the earth without a hitch had difficulty with the bump at the Pisces Club parking lot!

The Free Baba Movement

During my years in Washington, DC, one of the ongoing Ananda Marga activities was the Free Baba movement. In those days there were all kinds of movements to free protesters and political prisoners in the US, so for us it was not a big problem to organize a movement focused on getting justice for our imprisoned guru.

A few margis moved to Washington and set up a small Free Baba office in our center. They contacted the news media, organized demonstrations and even lobbied the US Congress, trying to get our government to take a stand and apply some pressure on the Indian government.

In this connection they launched a campaign to contact each and every US senator and member of the House of Representatives. There are 435 representatives and one hundred senators, so it was no small undertaking. They enlisted the help of various margis to go around and personally visit the offices of the senators and representatives and I was one of them. I went to several offices and recounted the story of Baba's imprisonment in India to the secretaries who were working for the congressmen. They listened intently, especially because we noted that Baba was being persecuted by communists and a left-leaning government in India. During those Cold War years, all you had to do was say "communist" and all ears would perk up!

As a result of this campaign, several US senators, including the former presidential candidate George McGovern, wrote letters to the Indian government asking them to review Baba's case. The organizers of the Free Baba campaign also informed me that several of my visits to Capitol Hill had been successful and that many of the offices that I contacted responded with letters to the Indian government.

In addition to the lobbying activity, the Free Baba campaign also organized big public rallies in Washington during the time that I was there. One of them came shortly after I moved into the jagriti. We learned that Baba had been poisoned by a jail doctor in India and that as a result he was fasting until the Indian government mounted a probe into the incident. Then a rumor came from India that as a result of the fast, Baba's physical condition was deteriorating. That rumor was all that it took to bring hundreds of margis to Washington to hold a public rallying bringing attention to Baba's plight.

Demonstration in Washington, DC, 1973. I am standing to the right of the monk, dressed in a sport jacket.

Our jagriti was a big two-story house but it was not capable of holding hundreds of people. We crammed as many as we could into the house and the rest of the margis stayed in places around the city that we had arranged for them.

In the summer of 1975, the Free Baba campaign organized a Universal Freedom March and again hundreds of margis poured into Washington to demonstrate on behalf of Baba. The march took place in the middle of August, when the government was in recess so it probably didn't accomplish much, but we margi participants were energized by it.

Despite the meager attention paid to our public demonstrations, the Free Baba campaign actually had some significant successes to its credit.

The previously mentioned lobbying of Congress was important, as were reports about Baba's imprisonment given by impartial and respected jurists and human rights representatives who were commissioned by our offices.

One of these reports was delivered by a Canadian jurist who represented the International Commission of Jurists. His name was Claude Armand Sheppard. He traveled to India during the time when Mrs. Gandhi had declared a state of emergency. He noted that Baba's trial was being conducted in an atmosphere of fear, because someone coming forward to testify on Baba's behalf could be subject to imprisonment under the Draconian provisions of the state of emergency in which almost all opponents of Mrs. Gandhi were stuck behind bars. He said that it was impossible for someone like Baba to have a free and fair trial under these circumstances.

Sheppard's report was delivered before a Congressional Human Rights Committee, and I was there in attendance along with a few other margis.

Can I Vote for You Guys This Year?

In 1976 I began to tour, giving lectures at college campuses and at Ananda Marga seminars. I spoke about different aspects of the Progressive Utilization Theory and how it applied to the economic and political situation in the US and the world.

At Princeton University in New Jersey, Professor Richard Falk, a well-known professor of international law, ran a unique seminar in which he invited representatives with different social and religious perspectives to give their vision of what the world would be like in the next one hundred years. Professor Falk was already in contact with us, contributing articles to our *Renaissance Universal Journal*, and he invited us to send a speaker to his seminar class.

I attended the seminar as a guest speaker, arriving by train where I was met by some students who helped Professor Falk organize his lecture series. We went to the university cafeteria to have a meal before the class. I was tempted to have some ice cream for dessert but abstained, remembering that Baba advised not eating sweets before a public talk or performance.

I spoke about the social cycle, the theory that history can be understood as a rotation of eras in which a particular class of people defined by their psychological type dominate each of the eras. In my presentation I traced a sweeping view of history showing how an era of survival-minded primitive humans in the Old Stone Age gave way to an age of warriors and monarchs, followed by an age of intellectuals and priests during the Middle Ages and then to the present period dominated by capitalists.

Taking my cue from Baba's book *Human Society*, I predicted that this present era would culminate with revolution followed by the establishment of a new economic and political system based on moral leadership. Professor Falk commented that he saw similarities with Marx's theory of history.

Professor Falk was indeed right but in my reply to his comment I did my best to show that there were important differences between my presentation of the social cycle and the Marxist view of history. "Marx," I replied, "predicted that in the last stage of capitalism there would be a few people with a lot of wealth and that they would be confronted by an angry mass of what he called the 'proletariat' who would rise up and overthrow the system. However, he did not consider that amongst the revolutionary mass there would be intellectuals and warriors as well as laborers and that this would have an important influence on the society that was built after the upheaval."

Prior to my visit to Professor Falk's seminar, a representative of the Baha'i Faith had given a presentation there, and due to this one of the students asked me if the leaders of the coming new era would all be Ananda Margis. From the Baha'i lecture, he got the feeling that the Baha'is believed that the future world would be a "Baha'i world" and that is why he wanted to get a better picture of what we were thinking.

I thought about the question and then said, "The leaders in the future will be diverse but they will be united by adherence to a basic moral code."

Another challenging campus visit took place at Bucknell University in central Pennsylvania. A margi student, Brian, was in his senior year at the college and was the main organizer for an event that brought a wide variety of speakers to the campus. Brian told me I would be speaking in the class of his political science professor who he said was a Marxist.

I was worried about how this talk would go. Though Prout does have some similarities with Marxism, it is basically a theory of economics and government that is dependent on a spiritual view of the world and this I imagined could cause friction with a hard-line Marxist. So I entered the class room with some uneasiness. Much to my relief the professor was friendly, and he and his students were really interested in what I had to say. Later in the day I attended another session on campus in which that same professor was giving a recap of progressive movements working in the US and he favorably mentioned Prout.

Another stop on my campus tour was the University of Rochester, in New York State, where a margi professor often invited Ananda Marga speakers to give talks to her students. On the day I was scheduled to speak, my acharya, Dada Y, was present. He whispered to me "speak about the six spokes of society."

He was referring to six basic factors that Baba said were needed to build a healthy society. I thought that this topic might be difficult to do in a university setting, but I launched into it mentioning the factors and giving examples from both history and contemporary events. The lecture was well received and I was starting to become more confident about presenting our social philosophy to diverse audiences.

In addition to the university lectures, I also spoke about Prout at margi gatherings. I was invited to a small Ananda Marga retreat in New Haven, Connecticut, and gave a general introduction to Prout. When the retreat was finished, I traveled back from New Haven to Washington by train and on the way I got another chance to see how our social ideas would "fly" with the public.

Seated next to me on the train was a middle-aged woman and we stuck up a conversation. She asked what I did and I started to tell her about *The Universal Times* and Prout. Since we were in the midst of the 1976 presidential election campaign, she was interested to hear about my political and social views.

"What's the essence of Prout?" she asked.

"We want economic democracy and government by people who are truly working for the well-being of the public and not for their own personal interest," I began.

"What do you mean by economic democracy?" she asked.

"Well, this year people can vote for the president but they may not be able to vote about things that directly affect their working environment," I began. "Suppose someone works in a factory and that factory is owned by a corporation. That worker has no say about who sits on the board of directors, even though that board of directors can decide to shut down the factory and thus terminate that worker's employment."

"How would you change this?"

"We believe that most enterprises should be set up in the form of worker-owned and -managed cooperatives. The workers would have a vote in deciding who sits on the management board and would get a share of the profits. They would be stakeholders in the business and this would increase productivity."

"But haven't such cooperatives been a tremendous failure in the Soviet Union and the communists countries of Eastern Europe?" she countered.

"The so-called cooperatives in the Soviet Union are not true cooperatives." I replied. "They are really enterprises owned by the central government in Moscow and managed by corrupt party officials. The workers have little to say about what goes on, so it is no wonder that these firms are notoriously inefficient. There is a professor at Cornell University, Jaroslav Vanek, whose studies of true worker-managed firms show that they can be more efficient than companies owned by corporations."

"But surely you couldn't expect all the enterprises in a country to be owned and run by cooperatives," the woman said.

"That's correct." I continued. "It would be best if the economy were set up in three tiers. Very small enterprises with few employees and dealing with non-essential goods and services could be run as privately owned sole proprietorships and partnerships—this would constitute the first tier of the economy. The guy selling peanuts or ice cream outside the park could continue with his business; however, larger businesses with more than a handful of employees should be organized as cooperatives. These cooperatives would make up the second tier."

"What's the third tier?" she asked.

"The large key industries with many employees handling transportation, communications, mineral extraction and other tasks that have a huge impact on the overall economy should be publicly managed either by a state government in a federal system like the US or by a public board in countries where they do not have strong local governments. These are the third tier."

I looked out the window and saw that we were already in New Jersey, but the conversation was not over. We were just getting warmed up.

"Wouldn't this third tier of state-owned businesses end up with the same inefficiencies as the enterprises in the Soviet Union?" the woman said.

"In the Soviet Union, the enterprises are not run by local governments; they are run by the central government in Moscow, which is often out of touch with local conditions. Their whole approach is to concentrate economic and political power at one point. The difference in Prout is that we want a decentralized economy in which regions would be able to develop in a diverse way, with a proper mix of industry, agriculture, and services. In addition, economic planning would be done at the local level and not in a distant political capital."

"It sounds good," she said as the train passed a blighted neighborhood beside the train track, "but how would you cope with poverty and inequality?".

"This is supposed to be the richest country on earth, and yet we have lots of poverty," I replied. "Ensuring that every single person has the minimum necessities of life is the duty of a healthy society. We cannot leave this task to the ups and downs of the market system."

"Are you advocating some kind of welfare system where everybody gets a monthly check allowing them to buy what they need?" she inquired.

"Not at all," I said. "The government can't just dole out money. That would just make people lazy. We need an economy that will provide people with jobs that will enable everyone to earn enough money to live with dignity."

"But why don't we have this kind of economy right now? All the presidential candidates say they are for full employment," the woman said.

"Under capitalism full employment actually means four or five per cent unemployment. Ask any economist and they will tell you that the economy needs some slack so that there will not be inflation. Some slack may be OK for the economists or the politicians, but if you are part of the four or five per cent that remains unemployed, it won't be OK for you. On top of that, what good is 'full employment' if many of those jobs come with salaries that don't give a person the purchasing capacity that he or she needs to get the minimum necessities of life. Clearly we can't go one with 'business as usual.' People talk about waging a war on poverty and about minimum wage laws and providing a 'floor' beneath which no one should be allowed to sink; however no one talks about a ceiling for the economic house."

"What you do you mean by a ceiling?" she asked, somewhat perplexed.

"It is the concentration of vast wealth in the hands of a tiny few that is behind most of the problems we have been talking about. We quibble about whether the minimum wage should be raised from $2.30 an hour to $2.50 an hour, but no one says anything about whether we need a maximum wage or a cap on total wealth accumulation. I think we need some kind of rational ceiling on wealth holdings, so that the gap between the poorest and the richest is not too great and so that wealthy people do not have a disproportionate amount of influence on the political system. If rational and moral people put their heads together, they can solve any problem that we are currently facing or will face in the future. However, if major decisions are left in the hands of the most selfish people on the planet, then we are doomed."

The train was pulling into Union Station in Washington so we had to bring our conversation to some kind of conclusion. I was not sure how well I had conveyed the Proutist view of contemporary events, but I was pleasantly surprised when my traveling companion said, "Can I vote for you guys this year?"

"We're not on the ballot this year," I replied, "but sometime in the future you will get a chance to vote for us."

4
I Become a Monk

EARLY ON IN my life with Ananda Marga I was ready to give up everything and become a monk. I was greatly attracted to all things spiritual, and I also enjoyed the good feelings that I got when I shared spiritual teachings with others. So it was not a question of *if* I would go to training and become a monk and full-time worker for the mission, but *when* I would go

As I got involved with the work of the *Sadvipra* newspaper and then *The Universal Times* and Prout work, it became difficult to extricate myself from my commitments and leave for training. My biggest problem was finding someone to take over my work on the newspaper. So I just continued working, but finally in the summer of 1976 I decided that I had waited long enough.

I told Dada Y to find a replacement because in six months I would be leaving for training. Dada found a team of margis who said they would look after my work, and I got ready to prepare for training. Shortly after my trip to New Haven, I moved from Washington, D.C., which had been my home for the past three years, to Philadelphia.

In Philadelphia I stayed in an enormous Ananda Marga center known as Baba's Castle. This jagriti had been a funeral home before Ananda Marga purchased it. It was old and needed repair, and with its high ceilings was hard to heat.

However, I was not concerned with the Castle. My mind was fixed on earning money for my ticket to the training center in Sweden, and to have some money to contribute for my upkeep there. I got work at

various temporary agencies, working in offices as a typist and sometimes in stock rooms. After a few months I earned enough money and was ready to go to Sweden.

I waited till the first week of January, 1977. This allowed me to attend the Winter Retreat. I had been to all the twice-yearly retreats that had been held in the US starting in the summer of 1971 and didn't want to miss the winter retreat. The retreat was held in Kansas and when the retreat ended I drove back with some margis to New York. It was very cold and the roads were glazed with ice but we made it back safely, even though one of the margi cars was involved in a minor accident. I now got ready for my big adventure.

There were five of us who planned on entering the training center and we arranged to travel together. First we boarded a plane for Frankfurt. While we were on the plane, I glanced across the aisle at one of the margi brothers in our team. He had the tray table down and on it was a bunch of chocolate candy bars that he was busy eating one by one. I was surprised because we normally didn't eat chocolate. Chocolate is a mild stimulant and according to the yogic classification of food falls into a category of foods that is fine in moderation for most people, but which was not taken at all by yogic monks and nuns. Also, those people who were working as full-time volunteers for Ananda Marga, with an eye on eventually becoming a monk or nun, did not eat chocolate products.

"What are you doing?" I said to him across the aisle.

"I'm eating them now, because once we enter training I won't be able to do it again," he replied.

We landed at Frankfurt airport and stayed a brief time at the Ananda Marga center in nearby Mainz. After a short rest we all got on the train and traveled to Copenhagen and from there to the training center, which was nestled in a small remote village in central Sweden.

The training center had been set up in Sweden in 1975. Prior to that time, all trainees had to go to India for training. However, due to the persecution of Ananda Marga in India, it had become difficult to train everyone there, which is why the center in Sweden was established.

The training center consisted of two houses, one for the nuns, or *didis*, and one for the monks, the dadas. The house of the monks had formerly been a theater and dance hall. Dada Dhrtibodhananda came to Sweden at the beginning of 1975 and with the help of local margis, he purchased this former theater and began to remodel it, to make it suitable for use as a training center.

When we arrived there in the first week of 1977, the entire village was covered in snow so deep it rose above the height of a car parked near the training center. Some of the drifts almost reached the gutters of the roof. Just after entering the training center, I went into the bathroom. One of the new trainees who had arrived with me on the flight from the US followed me in. The house was heated by a combination of wood fires and electric space heaters but we saw ice on the floors and walls of the bathroom. We looked at each other, and he said to me, "How are we going to survive?"

Somehow we did survive. There were fourteen young men in our training session. On the first day of training, the trainer called us all together and asked us each to tell our personal stories about how we had reached the training center. One by one we narrated our stories. When it was all over, I found it remarkable that although some of the details were different we all had pretty much the same story to tell: how we came of age, looked around and tried to get satisfaction in the mundane world and then were drawn like iron to the magnet of the spiritual path and finally to the training center.

Dada D told us that the main thing we had to do in the training center was to follow the schedule. The schedule consisted of getting up before five o'clock in the morning and attending sessions of collective meditation, classes, and self-study, concluding the day with chanting and meditation. It was a rigorous routine but it gave me the chance to read all of the books that Baba had written—at least all the books that had been translated into English up to that time.

We prepared our meals collectively, taking turns in the kitchen according to a duty roster. Normally we were not allowed any spices except for salt, but somehow the collective feeling and good vibrations transformed that simple food into the best tasting meals I had ever experienced. On festival days we were allowed to use spices and oils and prepared special meals that were also very good.

With a lot of meditation, chanting and study, the days passed quickly and the Swedish winter gradually transformed into spring. In the middle of the winter it got dark early in the afternoon. It was still cold in spring, but now we enjoyed more hours of daylight.

Sometime in June we were deemed ready to take our examinations. We had studied the conduct rules and spiritual and social philosophy of Ananda Marga, and also Bengali and Sanskrit. The most difficult part was to memorize Sanskrit poems called *shlokas*. These shlokas are verses from the various Indian scriptures (Vedas and Tantric scriptures and other ancient texts) that usually encapsulated a vast amount of spiritual truth in just a few sentences. Traditionally, spiritual teachers used them as a means to begin discourses on spiritual and philosophical topics.

Another important part of the syllabus was to memorize and to be able to elucidate the aphorisms, two-line couplets, in which the entire Ananda Marga philosophy was laid out. These aphorisms are known as *sutras* in Sanskrit, and the particular sutras that we were studying were contained in a book called *Ananda Sutram*.

It is a thin book with the couplets followed by a short purport explaining their meaning. However, the subject matter was vast in scope, dealing with the nature of consciousness; the relationship of matter, mind and consciousness; the Supreme Consciousness; the origin of the universe; the layers of the mind; the mysteries of life; death and rebirth; the nature of *kundalini* (the coiled spiritual force residing in all humans) and social matters in the last chapter.

That last chapter is revolutionary. Up until now, never had a book of spiritual aphorisms contained an analysis of how society evolved and how ethical people could use this understanding to build an exploitation-free society. But *Ananda Sutram* did all of these things.

I memorized the sutras and got ready for the oral exam. Our examiner was Didi Ananda Mitra. Didi was one of the first Americans to have been initiated into Ananda Marga. She was a Fulbright Scholar studying in the Philippines when she met an Ananda Marga monk in 1968. She eventually went on to write some of the basic introductory books for Ananda Marga.

I passed the test, and afterward the examiner verified my hand-written diaries, which contained our conduct rules and information that we would need to properly impart spiritual lessons to those who would be attracted to our path. That was July 7, 1977; the first part of our training had more or less come to an end.

I say more or less because to become certified as acharyas of Ananda Marga, each of the trainees would have to go to India to spend a short time at the training center in Benares (Varanasi). For me this wouldn't happen until January, 1981, but in the interim I was eligible to teach Ananda Marga meditation. I was given a new name, Dada Vedagarbha Brahmacari. *Veda* means "knowledge" and *garbha* means "womb." So one translation of Vedagarbha is "the source of all spiritual knowledge." In 1979, when I had personal contact with Baba, he elaborated further on the meaning of my name.

The First Lecture in Sweden

Now that I was no longer a trainee, I was ready to begin my work as an Ananda Marga monk but I was "stuck" in the training center. I received a posting and was supposed to go to Hong Kong Sector, the Ananda Marga designation for the countries of the Far East, which included Japan, China, Taiwan, South Korea, North Korea, Hong Kong, and the Eastern part of the then Soviet Union. However, I never heard from the Ananda Marga office of Hong Kong Sector. Without a ticket to the Far East, I had to sit in the training center.

By this time I was tired of the austerity. Meals were simple and sometimes skimpy, and every morning we marched to a nearby lake to take our baths. The trainer said we were doing it to save money on the utilities but I think he really did it to toughen us up and make us ready to endure in all kinds of conditions. However, at that time I was not thinking of "all kinds of conditions." I was remembering how my own acharya back in the US was able to fly to cities all over the country. Wherever he went, people took good care of him with comfortable accommodations and great food.

I think my trainer sensed my impatience. He suggested that I go to a nearby coastal city of Vaestervik to organize a lecture and try to teach some people meditation. When I got ready to depart, I ran into my first big problem: tying my turban properly. I tried once but it did not look very good, and someone suggested that I do it again before leaving the house. The second version was better and I was ready to bolt out the door.

Just as I was leaving, one of the other trainees suggested that I take along a portable tent. I didn't think I would need it but I put it into my backpack. I had to hitchhike since I only had a few Swedish kroner in my pocket.

There was no Ananda Marga center or Ananda Marga members in Vaestervik. Nor were there any contact addresses for sympathizers who might be able to help me. I was on my own.

The hitchhiking went well and I reached Vaestervik without any trouble. Once I got there, I adopted a plan of action that I was to use several more times in the years ahead whenever I went to a place without Ananda Marga infrastructure. The first thing I needed was a place to give a lecture so I went around the small and picturesque city until I found a small health center. I inquired if they could offer me a place where I could hold a meeting. They did in fact have a very good meeting room and said that I could use it free of charge, so I fixed the time and date for a few days later.

The next thing I did was to publicize the lecture. First I went to a local newspaper and asked to speak with a journalist. When I got in his office I explained that I was a yoga teacher and was going to give a lecture in the next few days. I got on the floor and demonstrated the peacock posture, in which I balanced my whole horizontally extended body on my elbows as my hands supported me on the floor. He took a photo of this impressive-looking posture and it appeared in the newspaper the day before my lecture with a short write up about the event. The next step was to get some kind of poster or leaflet printed. Somehow I was able to find someone who gave me free photocopies and also the use of a typewriter. I was able to make a basic information sheet about the lecture that I put up around town and handed out to people whom I met during my stay there.

When these things had been taken care of, I turned my attention to my personal situation. I had not spent any of my meager pocket money on transportation or on publicity for the lecture, but I needed somewhere to sleep and some food.

The health center didn't offer me accommodations to me so I had to find an alternative. I remembered the tent in my backpack and went to a campground on the edge of the town. I was able to find a place under a tree and set up this very simple tent, which was nothing more than a cord tied to a tree and attached to a stick in the ground with a piece of plastic draping over it to provide some covering. I had a sleeping bag and that was enough. I crawled into the bag and got some sleep.

In morning I thought I would be able to use the showers at the campground but when I got into the shower house I found that they were coin operated. They weren't expensive but it was beyond my means. There was a lake at the campsite so early in the morning I went to the lake to take my bath, just like at the training center!

Next I had to tackle the food problem. I walked around Vaestervik and approached some shopkeepers, inquiring if they had any food that they could not sell, either because it was expired or because there were blemishes on the fruits or vegetables. I managed to get some fruit, vegetables, and bread and took everything back to the campsite for a meal.

During my free time, I wandered around the city and talked to people, handing out leaflets to anyone who seemed interested in my activities. While in town, I met an Indian-born merchant who sympathized with me and offered me food from his shop.

Finally the day of the lecture arrived. About ten to fifteen people were on hand for the event, and I proceeded to give the first of many lectures in which I explained that human beings are unsatisfied because they thirst for infinite happiness but try to quench this thirst with finite objects. I explained that meditation helped one to move on the path towards the infinite entity, the Supreme Consciousness, and that the realization of the Supreme Consciousness would finally satisfy our desire for unending happiness and bliss.

One girl about eighteen years of age wanted to learn meditation. I think more people would have been interested but just before I left the training center, someone had given me instructions not to invite questions at the end of the lecture. It was bad advice but in any case, there was someone who wanted to learn meditation.

In those days Ananda Marga monks were allowed to give instruction to women, but within the next year and a half, Baba instructed us only to teach men. Women would be taught by the nuns.

The young girl came to see me and I taught her the process of simple mantra meditation. As I imparted the instructions I felt a tremendous wave of spiritual energy enveloping us. It was, I believe, the presence of the guru. I told her to close her eyes and start meditating, and I am certain that she also felt this wave of spiritual energy because when I told her to open her eyes, she looked like she was coming out of a deep trance.

So my mission had been accomplished—almost. After the lecture the manager of the health center said that I could stay there for my last night in Vaestervik. He also offered me some nice Swedish cheese and other delicacies. For one night, I got the kind of treatment that I had seen lavished on acharyas in the US.

The next day I was ready to go back to the training center. I had the newspaper clipping announcing my lecture as a souvenir, as well as a bag of fruit provided by the Indian businessman. It was a successful end to my first adventure spreading spirituality outside my home country.

I Start Work in France

When I was near the end of my acharya training, I began to think of where I might be posted. I had studied Spanish for three years in high school and one year in college, so I thought that maybe I would be sent to Spain or a Spanish-speaking country. Well that did not happen. One day the trainer told me that my assignment was Regional Secretary Hong Kong, and then for a few days I started to prepare my mind for that. However, after a short time, I was given a new assignment: Regional Secretary for Paris Region.

Paris Region is the Ananda Marga designation for France. I would be going to France to take over from another monk who was being transferred to a new posting. From Sweden, I traveled by train to Berlin. Paris Region was part of Berlin Sector, the Ananda Marga designation for Europe, and the headquarters of Berlin Sector was, at that time, in West Berlin.

The Ananda Marga office in Berlin was in an apartment with high ceilings in an old building. This was my first time in West Berlin. At that time it was a divided city and West Berlin was an island surrounded by communist East Germany. You could still see bullet marks from World War II on some of the buildings.

In the Berlin office, I met Dada Karunananda, the monk in charge of Ananda Marga activity in Europe. Ananda Marga was first introduced to Europe in 1969 by Dada Adveshananda but it really took off in the years 1972–1977. It was especially active in England, Scandinavia, Germany, and Italy. Young people of the hippie generation flocked to Ananda Marga retreats and many became full-time volunteers for the organization.

Our activities in France had only started in 1976 and there were few margis in the country. While I was in Berlin, a very senior dada from India was visiting the office. When he met me, he hugged me and later predicted to Dada K that I would be successful in my mission in France. Dada K told me about this but I didn't think much of it because I expected to do well regardless of anyone's opinion or prediction. At that time I didn't know that a high proportion of acharyas are not able to maintain their status as monks or nuns and that being a full-time Ananda Marga missionary is much harder than most people realize. I also wasn't aware that France was considered a very difficult place to work.

I was given a train ticket to France and one margi took me to the Berlin train station. I had to change trains but finally arrived in the city of Lyon, where the Ananda Marga's regional headquarters was located. During the train ride I did not speak to anyone and when I got to Lyon I somehow managed to go from the bus station to the apartment where the dada and three margi brothers were staying. The apartment where I stayed that first night was only temporary, as we would soon be moving to a large apartment in another part of the city.

Vishal, Ramakrishna and Govinda were the three Local Full Timers (LFT) who were living with Dada Vacaspati. Their job consisted of teaching yoga classes, setting up lectures, and assisting the acharya in social service activities and spreading spirituality.

After a few days we moved to the new apartment. It had previously been used by a French religious society called The Friends of Man and had a large hall that could seat up to a hundred. It had three bedrooms and a large kitchen. As was the custom in France at that time, we had to "buy" the lease from the previous tenant.

The apartment building was situated in what was called The Arab Quarter. It was populated by immigrants from North Africa, and though the area was run down, its oriental grocery stores, sweet shops, and tea houses gave it a colorful and exotic feeling.

As soon as I arrived, I wanted to get out and start teaching meditation. It was August and August in Europe is not a good time to organize any kind of activity as most people are away on vacations. The brothers told me that we would be doing a whole series of lectures starting in September when the vacation period ended, but I wanted to get started immediately. So I went with Ramakrishna to a busy pedestrian street in the heart of Lyon's shopping district and just sat there on the ground doing meditation. Ramakrishna stood watch while I was meditating, and when a sizable crowd gathered, he explained what was going on. When I opened my eyes I was able to talk with some of the people whom Ramakrishna had spoken with and a few of them followed us back to our apartment to learn meditation. This was my first taste of what was to come in the next five years.

Ramakrishna and I on a street in Lyon, France.

My First Lecture in French

When I arrived in France in the summer of 1977, you absolutely had to speak French if you were to get along. It was difficult to find people who knew English or would converse with you in English. I was going to have to learn French and learn it quickly.

Govinda and Ramakrishna, the native French volunteers, started me off on my French studies. We purchased the book *French without Toil* and Govinda and Ramakrishna recorded a cassette to go along with the text. I studied every day and did my best to learn this new language. I also helped prepare for some of the coming lectures in Lyon by putting up posters for the upcoming events. The first full sentence that I learned in French was, "*Est-ce que je peux mettre une affiche?*" which means, "Can I put up a poster?" I went around to many shops in Lyon asking if I could put posters for my coming lectures there.

One thing that really helped me to learn the language was traveling and visiting some of our yoga contacts. I spent a weekend with one man who lived in a city near Lyon. When I got there, I found out that he did not speak a word of English so for the whole weekend I had to communicate in French, which helped me to improve.

I was getting my feet wet with this language but I was not prepared for my first language test. In addition to preparing lectures for me in Lyon, some of the margis set up lectures in nearby cities. Three weeks after my arrival in Lyon, a lecture was set up in Valence, a city south of Lyon. One margi arranged a hall and put up posters for my lecture.

The plan was that I would travel down to Valence alone and meet up with a margi who was to translate the lecture. I made it to Valence by train and found the lecture hall. It was early so I did my evening meditation there. When I finished I was still alone. No one had come to do the translation. As it got close to the announced time for the event, people started filing into the hall and seated themselves. One woman even put a tape recorder on the podium to record the discourse. There was still no translator and I was thinking, "What is she going to record? There won't be any lecture."

The hall was full (about thirty people) and it was time for the lecture so I got up on the podium and started to speak in French. I am sure that it was not great French, but from time to time I queried the audience and said, "*Comprenez vous?*" do you understand, and they nodded their heads yes so I continued. Whatever I was saying was good enough.

At the end of the lecture, a young man in his twenties came forward and said he wanted to learn meditation. We went to his friend's house and I taught him meditation. Within a week or so he moved in with us in our center in Lyon and became a full-time volunteer for Ananda Marga.

So a lecture that I thought would have to be canceled ended up as a success. In the days ahead I would improve my French language skills. Baba himself was quite pleased with this and said so when I finally met him about two years later.

On the Road in France

My first big tour of Paris Region was done with one of the French volunteers, Ramakrishna. Lectures had been prepared for us in a number of cities including Poitiers in the West of France, Saint Brieuc in Brittany, Tours in the center of France and Grenoble in the French Alps, not far from our base in Lyon.

On this trip I didn't have to worry about giving the lectures in French because Ramakrishna translated my discourses. However, I had to get acquainted with life on the road, often making my way around France with little money and sometimes without secure accommodations.

We took the train from Lyon to Poitiers, where a well-organized lecture was waiting for us. After the lecture I was able to initiate some people into the practice of meditation. Ramakrishna also assisted me in translating the individual lessons, but he left the room when I gave mantras and other instruction particular to the individual. At the lecture we placed a donation bowl, and with the money collected we were able to purchase tickets to the next stop on the tour, St. Brieuc.

I am not sure who arranged the lecture in St. Brieuc but it was a full house. After the lecture I again initiated several people, many of whom were doctors and professionals. It was a big success but we forgot one thing: we forgot to ask for donations to help sustain our tour. So the next day we were without funds and had to get to the city of Tours where some university students had organized a lecture for us.

We did what I used to do in California. We went out on the road and stuck out our thumbs, trying to hitch a ride. But France was not like California of the late 1960s where hitchhiking was common. It was difficult getting rides, but we were persistent and miraculously made it to Tours just in time to give the lecture.

After that close experience, I learned one thing. Near the end of each of my lectures I would say, "The mantras that I give are free of charge, but when I have to travel on the train it costs money, so if you would like to help me continue my tour you can leave a donation in the bowl on the table in the back of the room."

The lecture in Tours was effective and again several people came forward to learn meditation. The next day we left Tours and triumphantly returned to our headquarters in Lyon. My first trip had been successful. I was new at it but it seemed easy. Later I was to learn that many people were enthusiastic to begin meditation but only a few were able to diligently continue the practice after I left their town.

A short time after this trip to the west of France, we were off again, this time to Grenoble, a picturesque city in the mountains, not far from Lyon. Traveling with me was Ramakrishna and a special guest, Dada K. Dada was a skilled lecturer and had built up Ananda Marga in Europe in the years from 1972 to 1977. Our lecture in Grenoble attracted many people, and Dada gave a great lecture that inspired several people who expressed interest in learning meditation. There was only one problem. We had nowhere to stay and no place where we could teach people meditation.

As I was to learn, the usual practice for Ananda Marga teachers in Europe at that time was simply to ask the audience if anyone could put us up for the night. However, this time we forgot to ask. The lecture had ended and we were without a place. Hurriedly we talked to a few people and one woman offered to put us up in her house. We told the people who wanted to learn meditation to come to that address in the morning.

All she could offer us was some space on the linoleum floor of her kitchen. Dada K, Ramakrishna and I had to lay our sleeping bags out in the cramped quarters, with one or two of us, directly under the table. Sometime in the middle of the night, someone else entered the apartment. It was the woman's boyfriend. He didn't like the idea of having three yogis camped out in the kitchen and told us to leave immediately. So we packed up our things and left the house. We waited outside till morning in that location because we had told the people interested in learning meditation to meet us there the next day.

In the morning some of the people came and we explained our predicament. One young woman offered us shelter in her apartment. She said we could stay there overnight and we could also teach meditation there. We taught meditation to a number of people and even held a collective meditation session in the evening for the new students.

Just as I had learned in St. Brieuc to be particular in asking for donations to help sustain the tour, I learned in Grenoble to make sure that I asked for help with accommodations. It usually worked for me, but sometimes I ended up with some unusual accommodations.

Rescued in Rouen

During my years in France I made it a point to try to bring Ananda Marga to places where I thought it didn't already exist. For example, once some margis from Paris organized a lecture for me in Rouen, a city in Normandy not far from Paris. They arranged a place for the lecture and put up the posters, but the rest was up to me. I had to go there by train, give the lecture, and hope that someone attending the lecture would be interested in learning meditation and would also be willing to give me a place to spend the night. That was the way I covered new territory. I never had enough money for hotels and depended on the hospitality of the people I would meet.

So I traveled to Rouen and reached the lecture venue, a public library located far from the city center. About twenty people attended the lecture, but as it turned out they were not interested in learning meditation or making deeper contact with me or Ananda Marga. When the lecture ended, the audience began to leave the library and I realized that I was not very successful this time. I got my things together (a guitar and a travel bag with my clothing) and started to walk slowly back to the city center. My plan was to spend the night in the train station and take the morning train back to Paris. As I approached the city center, a car stopped. A young man opened the window and said, "What movement are you in?" I told him I was in Ananda Marga and the young man replied, "So am I!"

I got into the car and my new-found friend told me that he had been initiated into Ananda Marga meditation a year or two earlier by Dada Rudreshvarananda, a French acharya. He also told me that he usually didn't go out at night, nor did he usually drive in the area where I was walking. But on this particular night his father sent him on an errand that took him there.

We both realized that this was "Baba's grace" and appreciated what had happened. He then arranged for me to spend the night with some university students, I was spared a night in the train station's waiting room and returned to Paris the next day.

Orleans and Dharmaputra

I experienced a similar incident in the beautiful city of Orleans. Once again margis from Paris organized the lecture. I traveled there by train with Govinda, who served as my translator.

The lecture seemed to go well. I spoke about the benefits of meditation and a good number of people attended. While I was giving the lecture, I noticed a young man in the first row who was really enjoying the lecture. He was positively glowing with interest. When I finished speaking, a number of people crowded around me asking questions. However, these people were only intellectually interested; they had no intention of learning meditation. One by one, they started leaving but in the meantime the "glowing" guy from the first row also left. At the end it was just Govinda and me alone in the lecture hall.

I told Govinda that there was nothing more we could do in Orleans and that we should just go back to the station and take the next train back to Paris. When we reached the station, we looked at the schedule and saw that there were no more trains back to Paris that night. So we went to the waiting room, ready to spend the night there. After some time I wanted to do my night meditation, so I went to the rest room to wash and get refreshed for meditation. As I walked to the rest room, I passed a café and was surprised to see the same young man sitting at a table with one of his friends. He asked me what had happened and I explained our situation.

He offered us a place to say on the floor of his small studio apartment, which happened to be right across the street from the train station. As it turned out, he was indeed keenly interested in meditation, and the next morning I taught him meditation, before taking the train back to Paris. That young man, who later took the Sanskrit name Dharmaputra, continued to meditate and was instrumental in organizing further events in Orleans and elsewhere in central France.

Food and Accommodations in Bayonne

We used to hear, via the Ananda Marga grapevine, various comments that Baba had made or was said to have made regarding a wide variety of subjects. I had heard that Baba once said that his whole-time workers would always have food regardless of the conditions. I never heard that he had said anything about accommodations. Both of these factors were tested when I visited Bayonne.

Bayonne is a city on the southwest coast of France near the Spanish border. One margi urged me to go there because it was in a region inhabited by the Basque people, an ethnic group whose homeland lies in northwest Spain and a small corner of France. He had heard, again through the grapevine, that Baba had said something about the importance of the Basques in establishing ideal regional socio-economic zones.

It was an area I had not yet visited. I had no contacts in the city but I wanted to give it a try since I was already visiting Bordeaux, which was not far from Bayonne. So one day I went there by train and decided to employ my usual strategy when I visited a new place: first get a room for a lecture, then put up posters, then visit a newspaper office hoping to get an article printed about the upcoming lecture. Once that was done, I would try to find accommodations for the night and leave the next day, coming back in a few days to give the lecture.

I jumped off the train in Bayonne and went to secure a lecture room. In France the city halls usually have rooms that are free for non-profit activities. I went to the city administrative center and sure enough I was able to reserve a lecture room for the following week. Next I planned to visit the city's main newspaper.

While I was hustling around I met someone who seemed to be the town drunk. He had a beard, long hair, and scruffy clothes and smelled like he had been drinking wine. He was quite friendly and offered me a place to spend the night. I asked him where his residence was and he told me that it was in the bandstand in the park! Many parks in France have old-fashioned circular open-air bandstands with a covered roof. This didn't seem like much help, so I told him that I would think about it. I thought I would be able to do better than spending the night in the park but I didn't say that to my new friend.

My visit to the newspaper office went well. I spoke to a journalist who said he would write an article about my upcoming lecture. Next I printed some posters and put them up at strategic places in the city. By the time I had finished placing the posters, it was almost evening and shops were beginning to close. I was so busy putting up the posters that I forgot to buy food and also did not get any chance to ask other people about accommodations.

After the frantic effort to get all the posters up I sat on a bench in one of the city's small squares. As I rested there, two young men came by and struck up a conversation with me.

"Who are you?" one of them asked.

"I'm a yoga teacher. I am organizing a lecture here in Bayonne."

The conversation continued and soon they asked me where I was going to stay. I told them that I didn't have a place to stay. One of them looked at my duffel bag and said, "But surely you have some food?"

I told them that I did not have any food. Ananda Marga monks are not supposed to eat in restaurants and I had no intention of doing anything further about the food situation since all the grocery stores had closed, but I didn't say this to the young man.

When he heard that I didn't have any food he said, "We are sailors on a ship docked in the harbor. We can't put you up for the night but we can get some food from our ship's kitchen."

They rushed off and I waited on the bench. Sure enough, they returned in a short time with some cheese sandwiches and fruit. I thanked them, ate the food, and then thought about what to do next. I decided to take up the offer made earlier in the day by the scruffy guy who lived in the park. I went to the park and saw the bandstand. The man welcomed me to his abode and I lay my sleeping bag out and tried to get some sleep. It became quite cold in the middle of the night and I had difficulty sleeping but then the man laid an old and dirty blanket around me and I was able to sleep the rest of the night. It reminded me of lyrics in the song "To Try for the Sun" by Donovan:

We huddled in a derelict building
And when he thought that I was asleep
He laid his poor coat round my shoulder
And shivered there beside me in a heap.

The next day when I awoke, I thanked the man for his kindness and went on my way. I left Bayonne and returned a few days later for the lecture. I taught meditation to one man who also offered me accommodations for the night.

From this and a few other experiences I concluded that deluxe accommodations are not guaranteed to roving acharyas, but I didn't mind because I enjoyed the adventure of going into the unknown and seeing what would happen. What I came to realize is that if you want to experience some divine grace and miraculous happenings, it is better to be insecure and go out on a limb in your quest to do something noble rather than sit at home with your good food and secure accommodations.

At a Europe-wide retreat in Italy, August 1978. I am the first monk on the right, wearing white pants.

Baba is Released from Prison

In the summer of 1978, we started to receive some good news from India. First, in July the High Court in India dismissed the case against Baba, which meant that he would soon be released from prison. Then on August 2 we learned that Baba had been released with great fanfare, including an elephant-led procession down the streets of Patna. I was elated to hear the news and knew that very soon I would get a chance to meet Baba.

After the celebrations had ended in India, Baba got down to work and started to give a new shape to the organization, emphasizing the role of elected District Secretaries (Bhukti Pradhans) and adding some new departments as well. I later learned that as soon as Baba had described the duties and responsibilities of the Bhukti Pradhans, he began to ask insistently if they had been elected in the various districts. Out of the blue he asked, "Has the Bhukti Pradhan of Grimsby been elected yet?" The monks in the Ananda Marga central office didn't have a clue to where or what Grimsby was but later found out that it was a fishing port in England where there weren't any Ananda Marga activities yet.

In late September, Dada K came to Lyon and gave me a long list of the new organizational instructions. He said that Baba had also introduced a new yogic dance. In 1971, Baba had revived Shiva's jumping tandava dance for men and immediately afterward the women of Ananda Marga wanted a dance that they could do. On September 6, 1978 Baba started teaching the *kaoshiki* dance.

The new dance was a moving yoga posture with sixteen different positions and was said to prevent twenty-two different ailments. Although the dance is particularly good for women, Baba also said that the men should do it too. I found the dance difficult at first but soon got the hang of it and began practicing it daily.

Baba in Switzerland

Now that Baba had been released from prison, my eight-year wait to see him was about to come to an end. Soon after his release, it was believed that he would soon embark on a world tour. In the spring of 1979 the world tour was announced and we were told that Baba was coming to Europe and that his first stop would be Switzerland.

On May 6, 1979, I went to the Geneva airport, which was not very far from my office in Lyon. There was an amazing scene at the airport. Margis from all parts of Europe converged on the airport and waited for Baba. There was an aspect of suspense because the passports and visa formalities of Baba and the Indian nationals who were accompanying him were completed at the last minute and those of us who were waiting didn't know if Baba was coming for sure.

Instead of biting our nails and just sitting there, we started to sing, dance, and chant the Baba Nam Kevalam mantra. Switzerland is a very conservative, formal place, so this spontaneous show of devotion at a busy airport was unprecedented. Several hundred devotees were singing for several hours, creating a festive spiritual atmosphere in the airport.

Finally we heard that Baba's plane was arriving. We crowded to the place where arriving passengers entered the terminal after having cleared immigrations and customs. I was still not completely sure that Baba was actually there, but when I caught a glimpse of Dada Ramananda, Baba's personal secretary, I knew that this was the real thing and that my long wait to see Baba was about to end. I had met Dada Ramananda in 1972 when he visited our office in Wichita. A second after glimpsing Dada Ramananda, I saw Baba coming through the crowd. He looked different than he had in the photos I was familiar with. Those photos had been taken before Baba's imprisonment. In the seven years of incarceration Baba had lost some hair. To me he now resembled Prabhupada, the guru of the Hare Krishna movement whom I had seen in New York in 1968 and later in San Francisco in 1970.

Baba and his entourage went to a small lounge area and Baba took a seat with margis, monks, and nuns from the various parts of Europe spread out on the floor in front of him. The Ananda Marga procedure for receiving Baba in an airport was to hold a special display of two yogic dances. The first dance was tandava. A few of the margi brothers, decked out in the official tandava uniform of green shorts and a purple singlet shirt, with knives and plastic skulls, began the dance. They danced for a short time and when they were finished Baba said, "Bravo."

After the tandava, the next yogic dance was kaoshiki. Now it was sisters' turn to impress Baba with their performance. For these ceremonial performances of the dance there was a prescribed uniform that Baba had introduced in India. For the women it was a maroon-colored Indian sari with a green blouse. However, when the instructions for the uniform were received in Europe, some of the acharyas felt that a Western uniform would be more appropriate. So someone designed an alternative kaoshiki uniform, which had a more European skirt-and-blouse combination. On the day that Baba landed, there were several margi sisters decked out in this alternative uniform and after the brothers were finished performing tandava they stood in front of Baba and started the dance.

After a short time they finished and Baba smiled and said, "Super bravo."

Later we came to know that Baba did not approve of the new kaoshiki uniform. He explained that there is a certain order to this universe, and that if even a small alteration was made then the whole universe was affected. He said that even if a small ant dies a premature death, then it has wide implications. In this context he said that the kaoshiki uniform that he gave should not be changed. In subsequent performances of the dance in Europe the standard kaoshiki uniform was worn by the margi women.

My Personal Contact with Baba

Following his arrival in Geneva, Baba and his entourage, consisting of ten people from India, went by car to Fiesch. Traveling with Baba was his nephew, Dr. Pathak, and eight monks and nuns.

Fiesch was a small village in central Switzerland with many ski resorts. We rented several buildings at one of these resorts. Baba stayed in one chalet and the margis were housed in dormitories. A large sports hall was used as the meeting place where Baba addressed the assembled margis. Several hundred devotees, mostly from Europe but a few from all over the world, were on hand.

The day after Baba arrived, he began his work. One of the first items on the agenda was personal contact. In personal contact, Baba would meet alone with a disciple. Often he would correct mistakes made by the disciple and then give a blessing. Most people experienced this as a transformative moment in their life.

As I was already an acharya and had not yet met Baba, I was one of the first people on the list to get personal contact. I am writing this more than thirty years after the event, so some details may be missing, but this is what happened to me: I went into the room and Baba was seated on his bed. I sat on the floor in front of him, and he said, "Be at ease, come closer." Then he asked me, "What is your name and organizational designation?"

I replied, "Vedagarbha Brahmacarii, RS Paris." (Regional Secretary, Paris Region)

Baba looked at me and said in a dramatic way, "Such a huge responsibility." Indeed, in India a Regional Secretary of Ananda Marga was someone with a big job, usually with several acharyas working under him and with various schools and social projects to supervise. However, in France I was the lone dada with hardly twenty margis in the whole country.

Baba repeated dramatically, "Such a vast responsibility," and then quickly added, "But you are such a little boy!" This was the Baba's charm. You could be an aged person with much experience in the world but when you came in front of him you did indeed feel like a small boy with a loving father. At the time of my personal contact I was thirty-two years old and thought I was already mature, but for that moment I was a little boy again.

Baba then asked me questions about my work. "How many margis have come here from Paris Region?"

"Close to twenty have come," I replied.

"And will there be a program for me in France?"

Shortly before the Fiesch gathering we began preparing a tour for Baba in other parts of Europe and France was one of the places that Baba was scheduled to visit.

"Yes," I replied, and Baba smiled. He was now reclining and looked like the reclining Buddha statues that I was to see a few years later in Bangkok.

Then with a lot of happiness showing in his face, Baba said, "And you are learning French." It wasn't a question. Baba knew that I was slowly working to master the language.

Out of nowhere Baba said, "Vedagarbha, ruler of the Cosmic Knowledge." When he said this, I felt like the actual "Ruler of the Cosmic Knowledge" was speaking to me, the syllables vibrated with a tremendous power, filling the entire room and the space around me. Baba was explaining the meaning of my name, not with mere words but with a real demonstration.

Then he placed his hands on my head and gave me a blessing. He said, "May spiritual success crown all that you do."

I gave him my salutations and left the room floating on air.

At the Geneva airport with Baba (on the right).

Baba in France

Not long after meeting Baba in Switzerland, I saw him in Lyon. Eight years earlier, I had a wish that Baba would visit our bungalow headquarters near the Pacific Ocean. That of course didn't happen, but now in Lyon I got my wish.

Prior to Baba's arrival we made plans how to receive him, his team of acharyas from Ananda Marga's central office, other monks from different parts of Europe, and the more than one hundred margis who expected to attend. The margis would be lodged in nearby hostels while the monks would stay in the jagriti. Discourses and meals would be in the large hall. A room was fixed up in the rear of the jagriti where Baba would give personal contact and also hold meetings. In an adjacent room, which housed our small printing press, we placed a portable chemical toilet for Baba's use.

Our plan was to have Baba stay in the jagriti only during the day and evenings. At night we thought it would be better for him to stay in a nearby hotel. We did not have a proper bathroom adjoining Baba's room, so some monks suggested that a hotel would be more comfortable. However, when Baba arrived, he turned these plans upside down.

After an eventful visit to Valencia, Baba arrived at Lyon airport on Friday, June 1, 1979. A large banner proclaimed in French, "Welcome to our Guru Shrii Shrii Anandamurti," and margis sang kiirtan as he arrived. The yogic dances, kaoshiki and tandava (with a live snake), were also performed at the airport. Baba was then taken to a hotel not far from the jagriti. Shortly after arriving at the hotel, Baba called a brief meeting of some senior acharyas (I was not present) in which he told them that it would not be proper to stay at the hotel. He explained that his presence there would disturb the other guests and then he gave them an ultimatum: either make the jagriti ready for receiving him or he would cancel the Lyon program and continue on to Italy.

The dadas at the hotel quickly called us at the jagriti and told us the news. We scratched our heads, wondering how we could set up bathing facilities for Baba? After a quick search in the courtyard of the tenement building one brother found an old iron tub, the kind people normally use for washing laundry. We put this laundry tub in the printing press room and attached hoses to the tap of the sink that was in that room. We then called the hotel informing the acharyas that we ready to receive Baba in the jagriti since we now had "bathing facilities" in the room next to the room where Baba would sleep and give personal contact.

Just prior to Baba's arrival at the jagriti, I peeked into the room where he would be staying during the weekend. Everything was in place: his bed, a *pratik* (the Ananda Marga emblem) on the wall, and his writing table. As I put my head into his room I felt a tingling—like electricity—vibrating through the room. I then went to the main hall, where margis were beginning to arrive. They were seated on the floor in long rows with a long tablecloth running down the middle of the hall. We were serving dinner to these margis when all of a sudden Baba arrived. When he passed through the entrance, which led directly into the main hall, the surprised diners looked up to see their guru striding in nonchalantly. Baba looked at everyone and said, "Continue doing your duty." He was then led into his room, where he took up residence in our humble apartment.

Once Baba was comfortably installed we expected that he would be ready to give a discourse. About one hundred devotees from France and other parts of Europe were waiting for him in the main hall. But behind the scenes there was another problem.

Baba called a meeting of the acharyas. We crowded into his small room and then Baba said, "I am not very happy with the work in Paris Region." He said this with a very sad face, almost like that of a little boy who had lost his favorite toy. As a result, there was no darshan that first evening. Collective meditation was held instead.

The only way that we could save the situation was to give a good report of the work that we had done in France, as well as credible assurance that we would do even better in the future. Since I was the Regional Secretary, the burden fell on me to provide the information that could change his mind, so I prepared the report. One of the crucial items was the list of district secretaries (Bhukti Pradhans). At that time our region was divided into thirty-two districts. In reality we hardly had more than twenty margis, since we had only recently started working in France. Dada K, our sectorial secretary, gave me some advice: "Prepare a complete list of all the Bhukti Pradhans, one hundred percent complete."

I used my imagination and came up with a secretary for every district. Then I submitted the inflated report to the Central Education and Relief Secretary. He looked it over, then looked at me and in all earnestness said, "Can you give me anything more?" Frankly, I thought he was crazy. I already was giving a report that was too good to be true.

In any case, it worked. The next day Baba began giving a series of discourses that were very deep intellectually but as usual culminated with the advice that merger with *Parama Purusha* (Supreme Consciousness) is the ultimate goal of human life. (These discourses can be found in the *Ananda Vacanamrtam* books.)

Along with the discourses, there were daily meetings. The acharyas crowded into Baba's bedroom where he took reports of our social and spiritual work. While Baba was sometimes very severe in his role as president of the organization, during his time in France he was in a light and loving mood. For example, he opened one reporting session with the word *école*. The Education Secretary was confused till Baba told him that this was the French word for "school."

One day, during the meeting with the acharyas, he asked Dada Dharmavedananda, "How many offices of your department have you opened in Paris Region?"

Dada replied, "Three, Baba."

"What, only three?" Baba replied. "Didn't you take the help of all those Bhukti Pradhans?" Then Baba looked directly at me and with a twinkle in his eye he continued, "I guess some of those Bhukti Pradhans aren't very active, are they?"

Later in a more serious mood Baba added, "Paris and Gibraltar regions are good fields but our action here was belated." He encouraged us to work harder to bring spirituality to all the people within our regions.

Field walk Along the Rhône River

In addition to meetings and discourses, Baba's daily walks were also wonderful events. I was fortunate enough to go on one of these walks. It was a cloudy evening and the walk took place on the bank of the Rhône River, only a few blocks from the jagriti. Walking with Baba were a few monks, Baba's nephew, Dr. Pathak of Patna, security personnel and about fifteen margis. We walked briskly along the river and then Baba asked, "What is the name of this river?" Baba's nephew, Paltou, who was then an adolescent, answered, "The Rhine."

I corrected Paltou and said, "It's the Rhône."

Baba smiled and said, "Yes, it's the Rhône."

Then Baba asked me, "Is the Rhône navigable for its entire distance?" I mumbled some answer but I really didn't know.

Baba continued the conversation and then asked us if we knew the Latin word for "water." Then he asked for the French and Spanish equivalents. Finally he turned to me and said, "Did you know that 1500 years ago French and Italian were the same language?"

We continued on a few more yards and then stopped. A folding chair was set up, Baba sat down, and everyone gathered around him. It started to drizzle and someone opened an umbrella for Baba. Baba was shielded from the rain but we were not. Baba said "Perhaps we should go," (due to the rain), but everyone said. "It's OK," and we stayed on.

Baba gazed across the river and it looked like he was peering into eternity. Then he looked at us and began to speak. I can't remember all that he said, but a few things stick in my mind. He pointed to the place on his face where the nose ends and the eyebrows begin (in yoga this area is called *trikuti*) and said, "There is a branch of astrology that explains that if one studies the structure of this part of the face, then one can know everything about that person." Then he added, "This is such a difficult science that even if I wanted to teach it, I wouldn't be able to find students capable of learning it."

The atmosphere was incredibly charged with love radiating from the margis to Baba and from Baba to us. Some margis were crying and at one point Baba looked at Devashish seated just in front of him. Baba gave him a tremendous smile of love. When Baba smiled directly at a person it was like no other smile that can be imagined—intense, playful and filled with love, stretching from ear to ear.

Then Baba said something of a very serious nature. He said that we have to look after the interests of the "less vocal" members of the human society, those people who are facing difficulties but are not capable of expressing their problems. Many years later I would write a song ("As the World Spins Around") about these less vocal people and our responsibility to them.

Finally our time was up and we reluctantly walked the short distance back to the jagriti, where Baba would give the evening discourse.

Personal Contact, Kaoshiki, Tandava

During Baba's visit to France we came closer to him spiritually. Due to the fact that he was staying in our small jagriti, we spent much time in close physical proximity to him.

Some of the big events of this visit were the sessions of personal contact (PC). In Lyon, part of each day was set aside for personal contacts. Several young men received personal contact, but one in particular remains in my memory. Normally, after the PC, the aspirants came out of the room with big smiles on their faces and then went somewhere to sit down and do meditation. However, one young man came out looking bewildered and sad. As he was my initiate, I was particularly concerned. So I went over to him and asked him what happened.

He said, "Baba told me to become a monk." He was troubled by this since he had no such plans or intentions in mind.

I said, "That doesn't sound right. Baba doesn't usually say this kind of thing to a person during PC. What did Baba actually say?"

The young man explained that Baba had told him to be an *ascete*, the French word for hermit or monk (ascetic in English).

I said, "No, Baba didn't say that. He told you to be an 'asset' to the human society." When he heard this explanation he came out of his gloom and brightened up like the other people who had received PC that day.

As many people have explained, Baba has a vast knowledge of many languages. During the personal contact in France, Baba spoke in English (and hence the confusion of the previously mentioned initiate). However, one of the young men initiated that day told me that Baba made him take an oath in French; Baba said the French sentence, *Je veux être un bon garçon* (I want to be a good boy), and had the brother repeat it. "How was Baba's accent?" I asked him.

"Perfect," he replied.

One of the charming features of Baba's visits to France and other places was the performance by margis of kaoshiki and tandava. It was performed at the airport and before each darshan.

Our jagriti was not on the ground floor, and the neighbors below were sensitive to loud noise made by dancing in our meditation hall. So during the performance of kaoshiki and tandava, there were only two or three dancers.

Before one of the afternoon discourses, there was a very unusual performance of kaoshiki. Dada Rudreshvarananda led the dance, calling out the rhythm with the mantra, and two recently initiated boys were trying to perform the dance, which is quite complicated for beginners. That day one boy was bending forward while the other was bending sideways; to make matters worse, Dada made a mistake calling out the rhythm. Still, when it was over Baba said, "Very good," with a big smile and everyone laughed.

Then Baba explained, "The foot movements were not correct, the body movements were not correct, and even the calling was not correct, but still I say very good. Why? Because I like to give encouragement."

The tandava dance was performed using a live snake. We had a small garden snake that accompanied Baba through several cities of the tour, including Stockholm, Rotterdam, and Valencia. During the performance one afternoon, Baba remarked that when one performs tandava "the snake must be venomous." He repeated, "The snake must be venomous." (This snake was not venomous, fortunately, for I heard that somewhere on the tour he bit one dancer who didn't hold him correctly. However, the snake, not the dancer, passed away during the tour.)

A historic moment

Within the confines of the Lyon jagriti, we passed many remarkable moments with our spiritual master. One event that took place at that time seemed like just another light moment, consistent with Baba's jovial mood during the visit. However, seen from my perspective, it was rather historic. One afternoon Baba gathered together the acharyas and told us that we would now have to start work in the communist countries. Up to that time our work had been concentrated in Western Europe. Our mission had started in Germany, went to Scandinavia and down to Italy and later expanded to France and the Iberian Peninsula. Now Baba was asking us to cross the Iron Curtain and go into Eastern Europe.

Baba started to give us some instructions regarding this new development. He said, "How will you work when you go to these countries? You will have to do everything subterranean." He put great emphasis on the word "subterranean" and as he said it, he made a motion with his hand. Baba was standing, but he bent over low and held his hand a few inches from the floor and moved it forward in a line parallel with the floor and said again, "You will have to do everything subterranean."

I had in fact met one family acharya in the US who had gone to Moscow in the early 1960s. He was there for only a short time but said that when people came to his house to talk about meditation, they were quite afraid and didn't dare to take their shoes off while they were in his apartment.

Then Baba said, "But there is one thing which cannot be done subterranean. Do you know what that is?"

Everyone was silent. Then Baba solemnly broke the silence and said the words, pronouncing each syllable carefully. He said, "Baba Nam Kevalam."

After that we did indeed venture into these countries to spread the seeds of *dharma* (spirituality). Despite any forebodings we may have had, our monks and nuns met with great success. As everyone now knows, by 1989 the mentality of the people of Eastern Europe changed and communism came to an end. Who can say, but perhaps our workers, taking their cue from Baba that day in Lyon, played a role in this transformation of consciousness that altered the map of Europe.

Baba's Departure from France

All good things in this world have to come to an end one day, and Baba's historic visit to France was no exception. After spending a weekend with us, Baba's departure loomed. But it was not without some interesting surprises.

Before I get to the ending, however, I have to make one observation. Baba really was at home within the confines of our small jagriti. The same jagriti that we thought was not fit to house Baba turned out to be much to his liking. After the last evening discourse Baba was in such a relaxed mood that he wandered out of his room (in the rear of the apartment) and moved about in the forward rooms. Dressed only in a t-shirt and lungi, Baba freely conversed with margis, who entreated him to please make another visit to the region sometime soon.

The next morning Baba and his team got ready to go to the Lyon airport. They were to catch a short flight to Milano, where the margis of Rome region were getting ready to receive him with all the love in their hearts.

I cannot remember the events of that morning, except for one. Sometime after Baba had departed I was in our kitchen with some LFTs. We were exhausted after playing host to Baba as well as the visiting monks and nuns and margis. The place was in something of a shambles. All of a sudden we got a phone call. Someone at the airport was calling us excitedly. "Baba is back," they said, jolting us out of our relaxation.

Despite having valid visas, Baba's party was denied entry into Italy and had to return to the Lyon airport. Apparently some instructions from a very high level were given to block his entry.

We jumped into a car and drove swiftly to the airport. A special expressway goes from Lyon to the airport, which is twenty miles outside of the city. When we were halfway to the airport we saw a car with Baba and his personal assistant, Dada Ramananda, on the other side of the highway heading toward the city. We continued toward the airport anyway to pick up the other members of Baba's team. After getting them, we went back to the jagriti.

Everything had been put back in order and Baba relaxed in his room talking to the monks. The French authorities had granted Baba thirty additional days' entry into France, but Baba decided to only rest briefly in Lyon and then fly back to India via Paris. We enjoyed his presence for that one extra day.

The next morning we took him back to the airport. As Baba walked down a ramp leading to the check-in counter followed by someone carrying a single piece of baggage marked "P.R. Sarkar," I marveled how one small, simply dressed man could have such a great impact on the world.

There are two more incidents of that day that I fondly recall. After Baba left, a few remaining margis went into his room and some did meditation there. That is understandable, but what really surprised me was when I walked into the room adjacent to Baba's (the one where we had put a portable toilet and a washtub bath) and found one margi sitting on the floor in blissful meditation next to Baba's bathtub!

I then went into the room that normally was my office. During Baba's stay it was Dada Ramananda's quarters. Now a few monks were there. Dada Dharmavedananda was exhausted and had fallen asleep. During the entire one-month tour he accompanied Baba everywhere, organizing the security arrangements and the field walks. He was sleeping but his mind was still engaged in the events of the previous days. He started speaking in his sleep and called out, "Where can we take Baba tonight for the field walk?"

I decided to answer him and said, "We can take him along the Rhône river," thinking that would be the end of it.

But Dada replied, still sleeping, "No, we can't take him there. He was there yesterday!"

We Get a "Farm"

The development of Ananda Marga in different regions is not a haphazard affair. In Europe in the 1970s, there was a plan for each region, which included setting up a regional office, starting a printing press and a business to support the activities, and getting some rural land where we could hold retreats and training camps.

We already had a regional office in Lyon with a small printing press, and shortly after Baba's visit, Dada K instructed us to find some land where we could set up a rural center. At first we searched in the east of France in the vicinity of Lyon but we didn't find anything suitable. Then one day Gurucharan called us to tell us that he had found an old farmhouse and barn on a small plot of land not far from Rennes in northwest France where he was living. An enthusiast for this region, Brittany, he urged us to come and visit.

I went there with Dada K and other margis. The two-room farmhouse dated back to the time of the French Revolution. It had thick stone walls, small windows, thick wood ceiling beams, stone fireplaces and an earthen floor. Thirty feet from the house was a large barn and next to the barn there was a tool shed. The three buildings formed a "u" shape with a courtyard-driveway in the middle. Next to the buildings there was an area where we could start a vegetable garden. The total size of the plot was approximately 3500 square feet, just big enough for our needs.. It was a peaceful setting, surrounded by rolling cornfields, and it seemed like we should go ahead and get it.

Since the land was small and the house was very old, it was modestly priced and we were able to buy it with the help of margis from France and abroad. Although the plot was quite small, we promptly started referring to it as "the farm." Years later, at the insistence of one margi, Baba named the project "Ananda Prasuna," which means "blissful flowers."

Almost as soon as we received the title to the farm, we began to hold retreats there, and in the summer months I held month-long meditation intensives and social service training sessions. A margi family moved into the farmhouse and kept the project running throughout the year.

One summer some monks from Ananda Marga's central office came to see our "farm." Dada K was showing them around the place while I was trailing a few steps in front of me. They were speaking in Hindi so I didn't know what they were saying, but when Dada lifted his arms and extended them forward and then made a sweeping motion all around his head, I caught on to the conversation. It seemed that the central dadas were asking Dada how much land we had. It was hard to tell since there were no fences around the property. So the wily Dada K took advantage of this and raised his hands to indicate that the adjacent cornfields were part of our holdings!

In later years I contemplated buying more land adjacent to ours but was unable to come up with the necessary funds. Despite its small size, the farm served us well. We enjoyed the retreats there and one of my trainees from the summer training sessions went on to become a long-serving monk for Ananda Marga.

5

Benares

*I*HAD ALREADY SEEN Baba in Switzerland and in France, but after nearly eleven years in Ananda Marga I had yet to visit India. After being encouraged by many friends and colleagues, I finally decided to go, and in late December, 1980, I flew to Kathmandu, the capital of Nepal, after having been told that it might be easier to get an Indian visa there than in the USA. When I published *Sadvipra*, I used to send a personal copy to India's Prime Minister. Since she was no friend of Ananda Marga, I was pretty sure that I was on the blacklist, the list of margis who were not to be allowed into India. Because of Ananda Marga's struggles with the Indian government, any non-Indian known to be a member of Ananda Marga was denied entry into the country. In those days, before widespread computerization of records, the enforcement of such immigration policies was not uniform and I was hoping that I would get a visa at the Indian Embassy in Kathmandu. My plan was to apply for the visa and if I didn't get it, then I would try "Plan B." We didn't call it "Plan B" in those days, but there was an alternative way to enter India in case my visa application was rejected.

I went to the embassy and completed the application form. After a short wait, I saw a consular official. He told me that my visa application was not accepted and then tried to get some information out of me, such as my spiritual name. When I didn't tell him anything, he tried to apply some pressure, saying, "You are supposed to tell the truth," but I didn't budge.

I had planned to enter India, with or without a visa, through the border at Janakpur, a town in the south of Nepal. I had booked a flight to this border town in southern Nepal but missed my flight due to the holdup at the embassy. In the end I had to take a bus to the border— the proverbial bus ride from hell. The bus was very crowded and the ride was long and uncomfortable. The road was full of holes and wound dangerously through steep hills overlooking deep ravines, gorges, and valleys. Sometimes these buses would skid off the narrow roads and end up at the bottom of these frightening abysses.

Thankfully my bus made it to Janakpur without plunging to the bottom. One thing I noted on the way was the contentment of the people around me. In the West, the conditions on the bus and its slow pace would have surely led to grumpiness and a lot of complaints. But not in Nepal. Everyone was smiling; even the babies and children on the bus were serene.

The bus stopped at various towns and villages along the way to let people get off and to take new passengers. At one stop, in a quite a big town, a man in a seat in front of me leaned out the window with an envelope in his hands. It was a letter addressed to someone in that town and he was trying to get someone to deliver it for him. Sure enough he found someone who took the letter for delivery. It was an example of the kind of cooperation and informality that is not generally found in the richer countries.

After ten or twelve hours, we arrived in Janakpur. I expected to see the lights of a small city, but there were no lights, just candles on the side of the road marking the places where small roadside stalls and shops were still open. When the bus finally stopped, there was no terminal, just darkness and some kind of parking lot.

I got out and went to look for a margi who could help me to cross into India. I had the name of one margi and an address. Well, it was not quite a real address as we would use in most parts of the world. I told the rickshaw driver to take me to the Shiva Sweet Shop, near the Janaki Temple, and sure enough he took me straight to the home of Shiva, a margi who ran a sweet shop near that city's Hindu temple. The sweet shop was tiny but there were about a dozen people working there—some washing dishes, others cleaning tables or doing various other tasks.

Shiva was a seasoned margi and he often helped people like me to get across the border. There was a formal border crossing where Nepali and Indian customs and immigrations people checked passports and visas, but there were also other smaller border crossings where Indians and Nepalis were able to cross back and forth without any formalities. For Indians or Nepalis, there was nothing unusual in crossing between the two countries at one of the smaller crossing points. People often lived in one country and had work or business in the other. They might also have relatives on the other side of the border. They were able to cross freely between the two countries without any monitoring system. I didn't look like an Indian or a Nepali, but I wanted to try entering through one of these informal crossing points since it was the only way I would be able to enter India.

Shiva put me on a truck headed to the border. After that I had to walk for ten minutes and then take a local bus-truck that went across the border. I curled up in blanket in the back of the truck and tried to remain as inconspicuous as possible. Somehow it worked and I made it across the border. However, when I got out of the bus and entered a small Indian village, I stuck out like a sore thumb. A whole bunch of Indian kids crowded around me, but I was able to safely find my way to a train station where I purchased a ticket to Patna, the city where Baba would be holding the year-ending spiritual gathering.

When I got on the train, I was in for another new experience. I didn't know how to get a proper ticket, since it was my first time in India and there was no one around to guide me. I ended up traveling without a reservation and so the first part of the trip was quite chaotic. At one point I was sitting on a dirty floor surrounded by passengers with big sacks of agricultural produce and other miscellaneous items that one usually doesn't encounter in passenger trains. The first train that I took, before changing at a larger station, was a rural train in poor condition and that was the main reason for my distress. After changing trains, things got better and I finally reached Patna.

In Patna, Baba was staying in a rented house. In the back of the house was a large tent where Baba held meetings and also gave talks to the assembled margis.

During my brief stay in Patna, a whirlwind of events took place and certainly I have forgotten many details, but some of the remarkable moments have left an impression on my mind which will remain with me till I part from this world.

I don't remember the discourses that Baba gave in Patna, but I do remember the morning his New Year's "Vanii" (message) was read out. It was the custom to read this message out in as many languages as possible. The reading started with the main languages, Bengali, Hindi, and English, and then continued in many Indian languages and in languages from other parts of the world. Since I was posted in France, they asked me to read it in French. I was shy because my accent was not very good, so I let another acharya who also spoke French do it.

The reading of the Vanii in all these languages created a tremendous spiritual vibration, a vibration of profound peace. Here is what was read on that day:

> Amidst endless reproaches and humiliations, profuse sweating and bloodshed, through the ordeal of unbearable torments and agonies, humanity has evolved to the present status. Nevertheless, it's your duty accelerate the speed of human progress. Your endless efforts to broaden and smooth the path of human movement will render your present existence and your future history inestimable.

As inspiring as this was, there was more to come. After the message was read, Baba left the tent and went back to his house. A few minutes later someone rushed into the tent and made an announcement. He said that Baba had given an additional message to us and he read it out: "I have seen your future, and it is brighter than platinum."

In another context Baba once said, "I am an incorrigible optimist." This additional message was an example of his optimism and his vision of a bright future for humanity, a bright future for those who were sitting in the tent in Patna.

In addition to the spiritual discourses and the delivery of the annual message, a major item of this gathering were the organizational meetings in which Baba would take reports of the work that was being done around the world. When Baba gave discourses, he radiated spirituality and love, but when he took organizational reports he was powerful and strict. His organizational strictness was meant to wake us up from lethargy and stir us into action. But even when he administered the organization with what seemed like an iron hand, he did it with humor and love.

I didn't attend all of the reporting sessions but one day after one of the sessions that I didn't attend, I was able to find out what happened inside the tent. Dada Tadbhavananda came out and said, "The whole session was focused on me." Dada was a powerful orator and a bold person, but like so many before him, he became like a little boy in front of Baba's commanding figure.

I asked Dada what had happened and he explained. "Baba said to me in a scolding manner, 'Tadbhavananda, do you know the difference between an idiot and a fool?'"

"I said that I didn't know the difference," Dada T continued. "Then Baba started to explain. Baba said that a fool has innate capacity to do something but doesn't do it, while an idiot has no capacity at all and can't do a task allotted to him. Then Baba looked at me and said, 'Which one are you, an idiot or a fool?'"

It is also to be noted that on other occasions Baba praised this same monk, saying that he was one of the best acharyas in the mission.

According to Shiva, the founder of yoga and Tantra, one of the functions of a guru is to both love and punish a disciple. The guru gives love but also gives discipline so that the disciple will succeed. The legendary story of the Tibetan yogi Milarepa and his master, Marpa, is a case in point. Milarepa (c. 1052–1032) wanted to receive initiation into spiritual practices from Marpa, but before learning anything he had to build several stone walls and houses by hand and then demolish and rebuild them. Milarepa's shoulders were bleeding from the work of carrying the huge stones. The guru gave this onerous task to Milarepa in order to exhaust the effects of the bad deeds that Milarepa had done before turning to the spiritual path.

Similarly, during reporting Baba was a fierce taskmaster who even wielded a stick. During this period Baba used to ask for the daily report of all monks and nuns. When I was in France I used to write the daily report every morning and then send one copy to our European head office in Germany and one copy to India. The reports were then consolidated and sent to Baba.

However, when you went to India and the reporting sessions there, you would sometimes have to give the report to Baba orally. One morning I was in the tent along with several hundred monks. Baba was taking the daily report. One monk of German origin stood before Baba. The general secretary asked him to give his report to Baba and all he could report was one word: "nil."

The daily report was a report on the work that an acharya normally does, such as giving lectures, teaching meditation, and doing various kinds of social work. Usually when monks or nuns from outside India would go to see Baba, they left their normal routine and only attended meetings and met people whom they hadn't seen in a long time. Looking at it this way, one might be able to understand that the monk standing in front of Baba might not have anything concrete to report. But Baba didn't see it that way. He became very stern and said, "What! In the long span of twenty-four hours he did nothing?" Then Baba gave the acharya physical punishment with his stick.

Although I only spent a short time in Patna, I enjoyed some remarkable moments with Baba. One day all the monks were called to Baba's house. Someone said that Baba was giving tantric *abhishek*. I believed that this was something like an initiation into the tantric family but no one really explained it further. When we got into Baba's house Baba looked at all of us and remarked, "What are so many whites doing in a sea of orange?"

He was referring to the *brahmacariis* like me and several others who were present, along with the fully orange-clad avadhutas. Brahmacariis are in the first stage of monkhood in the Ananda Marga order. A brahmacarii wears an orange tunic with either white trousers or a white lungi. Normally the tantric *abhishek* would have been reserved for avadhutas, but somehow Baba allowed everyone to be present and participate. In the tantric *abhishek* process, Baba consecrated spiritual energy points on each monk's body, one by one, with a light touch of his stick. I have never heard of Baba doing this before or after. It was something unique.

Similarly, a day later we were in the big tent for the reporting session where we were told that Baba would bless each monk one by one. We got in a long snaking line and then crouched down and approached Baba who put his hand on our forehead. After being touched like this, each monk sat in meditation and many appeared to be experiencing deep states of meditation. Finally my turn came. I crouched in front of Baba and he touched me on the forehead and then I sat for meditation. I could not feel anything at the time but was grateful for being there.

Some months later I was back in France, in the city of Dijon. I had set up a table to sell Ananda Marga books in the student union of the main university in that city. It was a cloudy day and my mind was also cloudy and downcast. No one was coming to the table to look at the books or to talk to me and I felt that I was wasting my time there. Then I remembered that my physical body had been blessed by the guru while I was in Patna, and my outlook changed immediately. After that, the sun came out and people started to flock to my table. A gloomy day turned into a wonderful experience.

Trying to Become an Avadhuta and Getting Something Else

Just before I had arrived in Patna, Baba had initiated a few monks and nuns into *kapalik sadhana*. This is a tantric meditation process in which the monk or nun does a special process that was taught by Shiva seven thousand years ago. This meditation helps a person to overcome fear and other mental bondages. The monks who practice it are known as avadhutas and the nuns as avadhutikas. Their uniforms are completely orange.

I really wanted to become an avadhuta. One of the young men who had been in training in Sweden with me was present in Patna and he had been one of the lucky ones to receive this special initiation. But I had not arrived in time and also I had still not completed the formalities to finish my acharya training.

Despite this, I didn't give up hope that somehow Baba could do something and give me the initiation right there and then. For that reason I used to walk close to Baba's house to see if something might happen. And it did!

One afternoon I was outside Baba's house and Baba's personal assistant, Dada Ramananda, opened the door and beckoned to me. He said, "Quick, get another overseas dada and come here."

I looked around and found the dada from Germany, the same one who had been punished by Baba for his daily report. We went to Baba's house as quickly as we could and Dada Ramananda let us in. He took us down a hall and opened a door and sent us into Baba's room. Baba was resting on his bed. He called us closer. I was on one side of the bed, the other monk on the other side and Baba was in the middle.

Baba started speaking. He said, "You both came here from long distances and had to go through so much suffering to get here."

We told Baba that it was not much of problem and that it was OK.

But Baba insisted. He repeated, "You both came here and had to undergo much trouble to be here and then what happened? Every time you saw Baba he had a stick in his hand." Then he said, "But look, there is no stick in my hand now." He held his hands out and then affectionately caught our cheeks and brought us close to him.

It was a very charming experience.

I Reach Benares

When the program in Patna was over, I went to the training center in Benares (Varanasi). Benares is a city along the Ganges that is renowned for spirituality. In fact, it has been called the spiritual capital of India. Our training center was located outside of the city in an old building that at one time had been a Moghul fortress.

Even though the training in Sweden that I had attended provided a complete course with all elements of the acharya syllabus, the rule was that one had to come to India to "complete" one's training in Benares, even if it was only for a short time. We used to joke that you had to go to Benares first and get sick, and only then could you become an acharya. And indeed, I did suffer from digestive problems while I was there.

The stomach problems that I got were probably due to the fact that Westerners are not used to the microbes that are found in Indian food and water. While I was at the training center, I witnessed a stomach problem that had another cause. One morning I heard a boy moaning. I peeked in a room and saw some of the staff rubbing coconut oil on the stomach of one of the trainees. They explained to me that he had eaten a large number of chili peppers the night before. Indians often chew on raw chilies while they eat, but even they have limits. The brother administering the oil said that coconut oil might help by cooling down his abdomen.

I stayed in Benares for ten days, after which I went to Calcutta where Baba and the central administration of Ananda Marga were staying. Baba continued to hold reporting sessions with the various acharyas who were present in Calcutta.

While I was there, I was officially given the title of acharya (though I had been working in that capacity since leaving the Sweden training center). On my last day in Calcutta I made my way to all the central secretaries (the heads of the various departments of Ananda Marga) to get my tour program signed.

Baba was a master of parliamentary procedure and formal organizations. Under the Ananda Marga umbrella there were many departments and sub-organizations. There were general secretaries, secretary-generals, chief secretaries, sectorial secretaries. It was complicated. When a monk or nun left the central headquarters to go back to the field, he or she had to meet with the department or organizational heads that had jurisdiction over his or her work. Since I was the regional secretary of Paris Region, I was in charge of all the various departments of Ananda Marga for all of France, and I had to see quite a number of department heads before my tour program was officially approved.

Finally, as I was about to leave, I met Dada K (who was also getting ready to depart from India) and he said, "Let's go tell Baba that we are leaving today." We went into the room where Baba was taking reports and conducting organizational business. First Dada K went up to Baba. They spoke in an Indian language so I didn't understand what went on. Next it was my turn. I went up to Baba and said, "Baba, I am leaving today."

Baba looked at me, smiling, and said, "And who gave you permission to go?"

I was thinking about all the secretaries who had just signed my tour program, but I didn't say anything more to Baba.

Dharma Samiksha: Unique in the Annals of History

After my first visit to India in January 1981, I didn't have to wait long for a second visit. I hadn't planned to make another visit but in the summer of 1981 we received a message from India saying that Baba was calling all whole-time workers (monks and nuns), as well as lay margis, to come to India for a review of their personal conduct.

Often in the course of reporting and organizational meetings, Baba would point out defects in conduct of monks, nuns, or margis. This kind of random review was normal, but now Baba wanted to systematically go over the merits and demerits of each devotee one by one.

As soon as I heard about this call from India, I made plans to go there again. We had just finished our summer retreat in Angers, France, and my schedule was free. Of course raising the plane fare for India for a second time in one year was not easy, but somehow I was able to purchase a ticket with the help of donations from margis.

This time I went to Bombay and not Nepal. From Bombay I took a train across India to Calcutta. This was before Ananda Marga had a big ashram in Calcutta. Margis and visiting acharyas crammed into a modest multistory building located in the Jodhpur Park section of the city. Margis were sleeping on the roof, by the sides of the building, and even out in front on the street.

Once a day Baba would come to this building to conduct *Dharma Samiksha*. Dharma Samiksha means "review of dharma" or review of the spiritual lessons. Later he would comment about this event saying that it was one of the most important events in the last fifteen thousand years. He explained that when various gurus came on this planet, they gave lessons and teachings but they never personally reviewed conduct and helped the disciples to overcome the bad *samskaras* (karma) caused by their previous misdeeds.

Baba would come into the small room set aside for meetings. If he was reviewing the conduct of monks or nuns, then there would be no margis present. Baba would be seated in the front, flanked by the one or two central secretaries. The person who would be receiving the guru's scrutiny would stand in front, a few feet away from Baba. Seated in the back of the room were the other people, some of whom would also be called up in front of Baba during the course of the session.

Baba would start the session by pointing out instances when a monk, nun, or disciple did not follow the strict code of spiritual discipline. He pointed out major lapses of judgment and conduct. Since this was done in front of everyone, it was often embarrassing. Baba would then administer punishment with his stick. Sometimes it was a light tapping on the palm, in other cases hard slaps on the back.

One thing that was important about these sessions is that Baba always ended each one on a positive note. For example, after Baba pointed out my mistakes, I felt really sad, but then Baba looked at me, caught me by chin with his hand and said, "Why are you not smiling?" My psychic pain vanished and I smiled.

Another common point in all the reviews was a personal prescription of yoga postures for each person. Normally the monks and nuns of Ananda Marga prescribe specific yoga postures for each student since each individual is unique and has unique requirements for achieving the best state of physical health. Monks and nuns generally inquire from a student about their personal health and then, based on their knowledge of the benefits of the various postures, choose a few for the student to practice. When I first joined Ananda Marga, my acharya gave me some postures to practice.

But now it was not an ordinary acharya giving the asana prescription; it was the guru himself. In my case, Baba said, "Stand straight and don't move." These are the same instructions that you get when you go for an X-ray. But Baba did not use any machine. While I was standing there immobile, Baba looked at me, gazing up and down my body as if his eyes were X-ray machines. Then he turned to Dada Vijayananda, who was by his side, and told him the names of some yoga postures. Baba named four postures in my case, and they have been very helpful to me over the course of the past thirty years.

I did not make a record of the various incidents during these sessions (though if you want to read some detailed accounts of this process you can see the book of my colleague, Dada Dharmavedananda, *Travels with the Mystic Master*). However, one incident does stick out because it was so unusual and because of Baba's witty handling of the situation.

I was sitting at the back of the room while Baba was reviewing the conduct of one Indian margi. The whole thing was done in Bengali so I could not understand what was going on. All I knew was that Baba was furious and gave strong punishment to the margi. Finally, Baba spoke in English for the benefit of the people in the room like me who could not understand what had just happened.

"This boy would go to a remote village and ask the villagers to catch and kill a big rat. Then he would tell them to roast the rat over a fire, and he would then eat the rat."

When I heard this I understood why Baba was so angry with this margi. But Baba's anger was usually momentary. It was something he displayed in order to make sure that someone had learned something from their mistake. Baba could change his mood in an instant, and as he was walking out of the room he turned to us with a smile and said in English, "Should we call it rat meat, or rat flesh?"

Dharma Samiksha went on at a hectic pace for a few weeks, and hundreds, perhaps thousands of people had a chance to stand in front of Baba for this unique type of analysis. But each time Baba reviewed a person's conduct, he was taking on some of the karmic burden of that person, and by the end of this period Baba became ill. After that he stopped receiving margis and whole-time workers. Thus Dharma Samiksha ended as suddenly as it had begun.

A Lemon Tree for Baba

In 1982 Baba introduced an addition to Ananda Marga philosophy when he wrote the book *Liberation of Intellect: Neohumanism*. I read the book and learned that *neohumanism* is an expanded form of humanism. In high school and in college I had been introduced to humanism, a philosophy that proclaimed that humans are the measure of all things and put its emphasis on the human experience on earth as opposed to speculating about what was happening in the heavens. At that time I was told that humanism arose as a reaction to the excesses of religion in the Middle Ages.

As I read the pages of Baba's book, I was introduced to a spiritually based humanism that included an ecological dimension. Baba said that when people expand their love to include all human beings, all living beings, and even all inanimate objects, then this is neohumanism. Instead of confining our love only to our family or our community or our nation or our race, Baba was asking us to expand our circle of love to include all, even the plants and animals. He also said that the key to attaining this kind of outlook is by doing spiritual practices, which nourish and renew our love for ourselves, for others and for God.

Immediately after the book was published, we found out that Baba wanted to put this philosophy into action by launching a huge plant conservation program. At his home in Calcutta and at the new Ananda Marga office building in Tiljala, an outlying district of Calcutta, Baba set up gardens. In these gardens he collected rare plants from all corners of

India and all corners of the world, both to save rare species of plants and also to educate us about the importance of plants.

How did Baba get these plants from all over the world? Every month representatives from the various parts of the world were coming to India for reporting. Now, instead of being required to only bring written reports they were also required to bring plants for the garden. This often posed logistical problems for those who had to bring the plants.

While I was in France, preparing to go to India with hopes of becoming an avadhuta, a dada from our European headquarters in Germany called me up and said, "Baba is asking for a lemon tree from France. Can you bring it?" I hesitated in giving an answer because I knew that there would be some difficulties. How would I buy the tree since I had very little money? How would I get it on the plane, through customs, and safely to Calcutta on the crazy Indian transport system? These thoughts were already going through my mind when the dada on the other end of the phone said, "Baba will be so happy to get it from you." That decided it. "Yes, I will bring it," I told him.

First I had to solve the finance problem. I immediately called a margi who was an ardent devotee and told him that Baba needed a lemon tree from France, and that I was ready to bring it but I needed help purchasing it. Without any hesitation he agreed to send me a donation, so that problem was overcome very quickly.

Next I had to find the right tree. I was in Paris when I received the phone call. After a little investigation I found out that there is a special district in Paris where many plant sellers offer their wares. I went to this place and asked for a lemon tree. I found one that measured three to four feet tall and purchased it.

When I got back to the place where I was staying, I had to figure out how to pack it. I had a big suitcase and thought about putting it inside. This would make it easier to carry and also keep it hidden, thus simplifying the customs procedures. Ordinarily you can't bring plants across international borders without special certificates and I didn't have time to get a certificate for the plant. However, it did not fit inside the suitcase.

Then I thought that maybe I could prune the tree to make it fit, but I wasn't sure if this would harm the tree or not. I called up the place where I bought the plant and asked, "Can I cut it to make it fit my suitcase?" But the reply was an emphatic, "Don't cut it!"

So, I just packed the tree using opaque plastic bags and tape, and went to the airport. I took the tree on the plane as carry-on luggage because I didn't want it damaged. Somehow I was able to find a place on the plane where I could keep the tree upright and in a damage-free condition, but more obstacles were waiting for me.

After landing in the Bombay airport, I went through immigration, collected my checked luggage and went to the customs clearance line. The inspector looked at my suitcase and then saw the oddly shaped plastic bundle that was "hiding" my tree. He realized that it was a tree, and started to get excited. "He's got a plant!" he said to his supervisor, who was standing nearby. The supervisor looked at me and looked at the tree and then nonchalantly gave a flick of his hand, indicating to the customs officers to let me through.

I grabbed my belongings and took a taxi to a bustling Bombay train station. It was teeming with people and as any visitor to India knows, or will soon find out, such places are perfect for pickpockets and other thieves. You really have to be vigilant in this kind of situation, and I was taking no chances with my precious plant. I had some time before my train would be leaving the station for the long trip to Calcutta. I was feeling hot and uncomfortable after the long flight and the trip to the train station. To my delight, I discovered that travelers could take showers in the station. I wanted to take a shower but worried about the safety of the plant, so I just took it into the shower stall with me.

The next challenge was to find a good place for the tree in my train compartment. Indian trains are packed with people and luggage and I was worrying about being able to find a suitable place for it. But as with the plane, I was lucky to find enough space for the tree and after the long trip to the other side of the Indian subcontinent I took my suitcase and plant and tried to find my way to the Ananda Marga center in Tiljala.

Tiljala was, at that time, an outlying suburb of Calcutta. In the early part of the 1980s Ananda Marga purchased land there and began to construct a large building surrounded by a tall boundary wall. I had never been there before so I just told the taxi driver to bring me to Tiljala. After the taxi let me out, I had to take a bicycle rickshaw the rest of the way to the ashram. I got on in the back seat, clutching my suitcase and my tree but we soon got lost since neither I nor the rickshaw driver knew the proper way. Finally however, I spotted the two Ananda Marga buildings. One building was the home of the Women's Welfare Department, where the Ananda Marga nuns stayed, and the other was the headquarters where the monks were based. Since this was my first time there, I didn't know which was which.

Before I could make any inquiries, a hostile man stepped in front of the rickshaw. At this time a communist party was in power in the state of West Bengal, and Tiljala was a communist stronghold. The Indian communists did not want Ananda Marga to spread and did whatever they could to harass our movement. This man, who may have been a communist activist or sympathizer, stood in front of the rickshaw and told me, "You don't have a visa to come and stay with AMPS." (AMPS is the acronym for Ananda Marga Pracaraka Samgha, the formal name of the organization.) I looked at him and quickly decided that I did not want to get into any kind of argument. I grabbed my suitcase and my plant and jumped off the rickshaw and dashed to the closest Ananda Marga structure. The door opened and I entered, feeling relief from the tension of not knowing where I was going and then having to confront the menacing man.

It turned out that I had entered the Women's Welfare Department compound, but after a short time I was safely escorted to the compound where Baba conducted the reporting sessions. This was the place where I would be staying. As soon as I got inside the compound, I found my assigned room and was told where I could deposit my plant. One monk was in charge of the plants. He had a register in which he entered the type of plant and the name of the person who brought it.

The next day I met this monk again and he told me that he had given it to Baba. This is how he explained it to me: Baba asked him, "Who brought this?" The monk gave my name in reply and then Baba commented, "Oh, he speaks French." And then Baba looked at the plant and said, "But how did he get it here?"

The story of the plant didn't end there. One night I was at Baba's residence in Lake Gardens, a residential, middle-class area of Calcutta where we purchased a house for Baba shortly after he came out of prison. In the early 1980s, the Lake Gardens house was Baba's principal residence. He gave discourses in main hall of the house on Sundays and also conducted organizational reporting sessions there. That night I was called to go on the field walk with Baba. Baba got into his car and sat in the back seat with Dada Vijayananda, a senior monk who translated many of Baba's books from Bengali into English. I rode in the jeep that followed Baba's car, together with the security personnel.

We drove to a nearby lake. We got out of the vehicles and started walking on a path that wound its way around the lake. Baba was walking ahead, talking to Dada Vijayananda, and I was with the security people, trailing behind about twenty feet or so. Then Baba slowed down and after a few steps we were just behind him. He turned around and said, "Where is my Vedagarbha?" I popped out of the darkness right in front of Baba. Baba looked at me with a big smile and said, "You brought me a nice present."

A Romantic Ending

My stay in India also included my first visit to Ananda Nagar, the City of Bliss.

During the 1980s much of the central administration of Ananda Marga was conducted in Calcutta, which was where Baba spent much of his time. However the official headquarters of Ananda Marga was in a rural spiritual social service complex that Baba named Ananda Nagar.

Ananda Nagar is spread out over a vast area of land in West Bengal. The land was donated to Ananda Marga by a former Maharaja, and Ananda Marga first started work there in the early 1960s. Soon monks and nuns set up many educational and social service projects at Ananda Nagar and for a brief time in early 1967 Baba resided there. In Ananda Nagar the organization operates all levels of schools, ranging from a degree college to kindergartens, children's homes, a hospital, farming projects and industries. Baba took much interest in the development of Ananda Nagar because he wanted it to help bring about an economic and cultural renaissance in India's impoverished rural areas. He proudly said, "I am the Anandamurti of Ananda Nagar."

We used to visit Ananda Nagar regularly in the 1980s, especially during the New Year's holiday when the *Dharma Maha Cakra* (great spiritual gathering) was held. Baba would give several discourses during this event, including a special spiritual discourse that would culminate with him giving *varabhaya mudra*, a positioning of hands in which he conveyed blessings and generated waves of spiritual energy.

The Dharma Maha Cakra (DMC) was a festive event. People came from all over India and all over the world. But since this was a rural setting, the accommodations and the amenities were very rustic. We used to take our bath either at a well, drawing the water from buckets and splashing it over ourselves with a plastic mug, or at the small river that ran through the central portion of Ananda Nagar. There was no hot water tap and the water could be rather cold.

Devotees stand in front of Baba's house in Ananda Nagar. The monk in the center is Dada Ishvarakrsnananda. I am to his right.

One morning before the DMC's main events were to begin, Baba went on a tour of the facility to see how everyone was doing. He greeted us like a father welcoming the whole family to his house. He said, "I hope that you are all comfortable." He said that the water is cold, but quipped, "when you take a bath here you accomplish your *Bhuta Shuddhi*." Bhuta Shuddhi is the first step of the meditation process in which you try to forget about the outside physical surroundings. And, indeed, when you poured that cold Ananda Nagar water on yourself on a late December morning, you would begin to withdraw from all other sensory stimulation.

Another feature of our visits to Ananda Nagar in the 1980s was the cat-and-mouse game that we had to play with the local police. The communist government of West Bengal wanted to wipe out Ananda Marga. In fact, on April 30, 1982, seventeen monks and nuns were slaughtered in the streets of Calcutta by a mob that most people believe was led by communist activists. At Ananda Nagar, local police surrounded the area and tried to find foreigners and then detain them to get their identification information, which would be added to a government blacklist that was used to bar members of Ananda Marga from entering India. Sometimes detained foreigners were summarily deported.

With this in mind, special arrangements were made for the departure of margis who had come from abroad. In the middle of the night we were crammed into a large truck that was closed so that no one could see what or who was inside. We were so jammed in, it was not a pleasant feeling. After a short while the truck broke down, and much to my relief, we had to get out. It was the middle of the night and someone led us from there on foot. We walked for several miles until we crossed the border into the neighboring state of Bihar, where there was no police or state vendetta against Ananda Marga. There we boarded buses back to Calcutta.

We took this all in stride. After arriving back in Calcutta, we got refreshed and then went to Baba's residence in Lake Gardens. On our first morning back in Calcutta, Baba came out of his house for his morning walk and greeted us. Then he said, "I think that everyone enjoyed their stay at Ananda Nagar." Then with a smile he added, "But the ending was a bit romantic."

After the "romance" of Ananda Nagar and my India visit, I returned to France to resume my touring and lecturing.

We Start a Granola Business

Compared to the other parts of Europe, Ananda Marga in France was still underdeveloped. In Germany, Italy, Scandinavia, England, and even Iceland the Ananda Marga centers were supported by bustling businesses. For the most part, these businesses were health-food shops, and in Italy, England, and Iceland there were also food production enterprises. Ananda Marga introduced peanut butter to Italy when one margi started a small plant making nut butters and other health foods. Ananda Marga's Peace Eye health-food stores in Berlin were also among the first stores of this kind in the country.

We didn't have anything like that in France and I was wondering how we could catch up. As I was leaving the US in 1976, I noticed that some people were producing fruit-and-nut bars and thought that maybe we could do something like that in France. Thinking about those bars, I went to the large Middle Eastern grocery below our jagriti and purchased some dried fruit and nuts and made some prototypes. I even made a hand-drawn colorful label naming the product as an "Ananda Bar." The prototype was wrapped with clear plastic and it looked "real." I showed it to the business-minded Dada K and he loved it.

However, I still had to go from the prototype to actual production. While I was thinking how to do this, I also experimented in the kitchen with a batch of granola, the toasted oat breakfast cereal that seemed to come from nowhere when the hippie movement began in the late 1960s. I showed the Ananda Bar and the granola to the LFTs in Lyon and Vishal suggested that we should try to start a granola business.

We started out making it in the oven of our kitchen stove and after a few months got an industrial pizza oven, which we installed in our rather large kitchen. The brand name was Vijaya, which means permanent victory. In the US some margis had started an incense-making business with the name Jaya, which means victory. I thought we should make sure that we came out on top so I opted for permanent victory in our brand name.

We packaged the granola in transparent bags, put on our labels and we were in business. Soon we were delivering granola to close to twenty stores in Lyon. There were of course a number of obstacles that we had to overcome. First of all, French people at that time didn't eat big breakfasts as they do in the US or in England, and they generally didn't eat breakfast cereals. Secondly they had never heard of granola. We introduced the product in any case and people liked it; some of them who didn't eat a traditional breakfast just munched on it as a snack food.

The biggest problem however was quality control. Our kitchen was not a dedicated factory and our volunteers had many other things to do in addition to making granola. Also the oven was not quite suited to the job—if the batch was left in the oven a few seconds too long, it could burn. We used to eat the slightly burnt granola for breakfast, and indeed we had plenty of breakfasts with it.

We carried on for quite a while but one day we did some sober accounting and found out that our income equaled what we spent on ingredients, electricity for the oven, and the upkeep of our small car. It was clearly not a profitable business so we eventually phased it out.

Lyon is not just any city in France. It is an important commercial center, and though it vied with Marseilles as the second largest city in France, it is second to none in the field of gastronomy with its restaurants and chefs regarded as the best in the country and even the world. Years later, when I told the story of how we introduced granola in Lyon to a professional chef in the US, he simply smiled and shook my hand!

The Wisdom of Yoga

When I was working France, we had a big problem: we did not have books in French about Ananda Marga philosophy. We did print a book on the spiritual practices (*The 16 Points*) and Baba's *Guide to Human Conduct*, which addresses ethics, but we didn't have a French-language book that offered a comprehensive look at Ananda Marga's philosophy.

Lokesh, a young man from the west of France who was working with me, kept saying, "Dada, we don't have books in French; we need some as soon as possible." So, I got out our old manual typewriter and started working on a book.

First I wrote a chapter on Tantra, because this subject is badly misunderstood in the West. Tantra is the name given to the fundamental spiritual practices that originated in India more than seven thousand years ago. The yoga of today is based on this system of spiritual practice. Similarly, the very popular forms of Tibetan Buddhism that are now widely taught in the West also have tantric roots. However, due to the confusion that resulted from the misinterpretation of these practices, Tantra is sometimes seen as a dark practice concerned with occult powers or debauched behavior. As Ananda Marga is essentially Tantra for the modern age, I felt that it was important to explain the origins and essentials of this ancient practice.

No sooner had I finished typing the first chapter when Lokesh snatched the pages out of my hand and started translating them into French. I immediately started working on the next chapter, *ashtanga* yoga, the eight parts of yoga that lead a person to true fulfillment. Lokesh again took the pages away from me and translated them into French. I subsequently wrote chapters on yoga cosmology, reincarnation, layers of the mind, and the social philosophy of Ananda Marga (Neohumanism and the Progressive Utilization Theory). By the time we were finished, we had a book that gave a concise look at Ananda Marga philosophy. We called it *The Wisdom of Tantra*. In later editions in English and other languages it became *The Wisdom of Yoga*. Although it was written in 1982 to fulfill an immediate pressing need, the book is still being used to give people the explanations they need before getting into Baba's books, many of which assume that you are familiar with the basic concepts of Ananda Marga philosophy.

The Best Job in the World

The life of an Ananda Marga monk or nun is up and down. We don't get a salary from our central office and we do not have the kind of security that people with more conventional occupations enjoy. At one moment we may be living in favorable circumstances and at another moment we might be homeless. But despite these uncertainties there were and are fringe benefits that most people never get to enjoy.

During the early 1980s, the summer retreats of Ananda Marga in Europe were held in France. In 1980 we held a retreat in Brittany (near Rennes) in a school that was on summer vacation. In 1981 we held the retreat in an old Chateau near Angers (in Northwest France). However, we did not have a fixed place to hold the summer retreat in 1982, and since I was the person in charge for operations in France, I was the one who had to come up with a new retreat location.

At this time, I was nearing the end of my stay in France. Another monk was working with me, getting ready to take over from me. His name was Dada Rudreshvarananda and he was a native Frenchman, from Perpignan in the south of the country. When we were given instructions to find the retreat site for 1982, we eventually narrowed our search down to a village called Tourrettes-sur-Loup, which is located in the southeast of the country, near the city of Nice.

Nice is aptly named as it is a very nice city! It is on the Mediterranean Sea and has a wonderful climate. I haven't been there in many years but I remember the flowerpots and colorful geraniums decorating the city's houses. Even more beautiful was the surrounding countryside, where our hoped-for retreat site was located. We had the address and knew that it was located in the mountainous area northwest of Nice. We did not have a car and it was in an area that was not covered by a regular bus service but we somehow managed to hitchhike there. Our last ride was in a farmer's old pickup truck that took us directly to the site. Dada Rudreshvarananda and I were sitting in the back of the open truck as it wound its way up the curving mountainous road. We marveled at the beautiful scenery. All around us were hills dotted with small farms, and as we gazed southward we could see the deep blue of the Mediterranean Sea. Dada looked at the scenery and then turned to me and said, "We have the best job in the world."

6

The Far East and Back

On September 18, 1982 I departed from France and headed to the Far East, or what Ananda Marga calls Hong Kong Sector. I had been in France for more than five years, and in that time I had given countless lectures in every part of the country. During that period, I had also given personal lessons in meditation to over seven hundred people.

Actually, I had been designated for transfer to Hong Kong Sector almost two years earlier, but the transfer was not completed because I was not sent a ticket, nor was a replacement sent to take over my activities in France. To be honest, in 1980 I didn't want to leave France because I was just getting started there, so I didn't make any extraordinary effort to go to my new post. However, by 1982 I was quite happy to leave and take on a new challenge.

Hong Kong Sector comprises China, the eastern part of the then Soviet Union (from the Urals to the Pacific), Japan, Hong Kong, Taiwan and Korea. At the time we did not have any activities in the communist parts of the sector and our main offices were in Hong Kong, Taiwan, Japan, and Korea.

My first stop was in Hong Kong. Hong Kong is a bustling metropolis, one of the most densely populated cities of the world. It has a tropical climate and when I got there it was hot and humid. I had to take a cold bath four times a day in order to feel comfortable. Our Ananda Marga center at that time was in an apartment in downtown Hong Kong and from the windows of the apartment you could hear the constant noise of ongoing construction, complete with swinging cranes and deafening jackhammers. The heat and the noise were unbearable and I thought, "If I can't do meditation here, then what about the people who might become my students?"

While I was in Hong Kong I connected with a young Chinese man whom I had initiated in Orleans. I also was a guest at some yoga classes taught by one of the margis. But otherwise, I was not able to do much in my short time there.

After a few weeks, I went on to Taipei, which was the headquarters of Ananda Marga in the Far East. There were a lot of margis in Taipei and also in other cities of Taiwan. They enjoyed coming to our centers whenever they could, and the jagritis were alive with energy. I gave some lectures in Taipei and initiated some young men into meditation practice. I also had a chance to visit Ananda Marga centers in Hsinchu and Kaohsiung.

When I reached Hong Kong Sector, my posting was the sectorial PCAP secretary. PCAP is an acronym that stands for "Prevention of Cruelty to Animals and Plants." You can say that it is the ecological section of Ananda Marga. Once I knew what my new designation was, I got busy and put together a newsletter for the PCAP department. The feature article was about tropical forest destruction. I sent it to the PCAP secretary in India and he was really pleased with it.

I would have been happy to be the PCAP secretary in the Far East, but the head monk of the Sector wanted me to become the sectorial office secretary in our headquarters in Taipei. The term office secretary doesn't sound like much but it is a key administrative position. This secretary has to maintain communication with the monks and nuns and lay members of Ananda Marga, send reports to India, and also do the financial accounts.

A few weeks after I set up my office in Taipei, a new sectorial secretary was posted and he wanted us to move the office to Japan in order to enhance Ananda Marga's presence there. Soon I was on my way to Japan.

Unlike Taiwan, in Japan there were not a lot of margis. There were a lot of monks and a few nuns, but very few margis. The lack of dedicated lay members caused a lot of material problems for the monks and nuns who were working in Japan. There were no donations and in order to sustain themselves, they set up yoga classes and also tried begging door to door in the style of Japanese Buddhist monks. When I reached Japan in January 1983, they had discovered a new income stream. One of the monks met a French expatriate living in Tokyo and taught him meditation. This Frenchman was importing cheap oil paintings from Hong Kong and selling them in the subway station corridors. He would set them up on easels and sell them to Japanese businessmen, especially in the evening when the businessmen would stagger home after a long day of work and a few hours of drinking.

The inebriated businessmen were flush with cash and it was possible to sell some of the paintings for ten times their import price. Our enterprising dada got his very own stock of paintings and went out to the subway stations with great success. Soon I joined him, along with a few other colleagues. Six evenings a week we went out to sell oil paintings.

With a secure income, we could think about renting a proper apartment for our activities. I went around Tokyo with one dada who was fluent in Japanese and we found an apartment located on the tenth floor of a modern building in the Honancho section of Tokyo. The apartment was perfectly laid out for our activities. Just inside the entrance corridor, to the right, was a small room that we chose to be our office area. The biggest room was a long and spacious with tatami mats made out of bamboo. There was also another small room with tatami mats. During the night we rolled out our sleeping bags and during the day they were neatly tucked away in closets. The whole apartment, especially the main room, had a nice, peaceful look, perfect for yoga and meditation and vegetarian dinners. We just had to figure out how to attract people to the premises.

We continued selling paintings in the evenings and had more than enough money to pay our rent and purchase proper food. But our financial goals were more ambitious than that. We decided to pool our funds so that we could purchase some land in Japan. We went to a local bank to set up an account and I told the bank manager, "We are going to deposit thirty million yen in this account."

We eventually reached our target and bought land near Narita airport just outside of Tokyo, though I was no longer in Japan when this happened.

Concerts in the Tokyo Jagriti

Having a spacious office in Tokyo offered us an opportunity to host some interesting programs, as well as providing us with a base from which we could raise money for our land project. Now it was just a question of finding programs that would be attractive to the Japanese.

When I was in Europe I had heard of full-moon festivals that some margis had organized. Musicians and artists would perform and the guests enjoyed vegetarian refreshments and socialized after the performances. These programs were usually held in the intimate settings of our yoga centers rather than in large rented concert halls.

I wanted to try something like this in Tokyo in our new apartment. I was starting from scratch so the first musicians that I was able to enlist were Dada Vibhuti Bushan and me! Dada Vibhuti Bushan was Italian and he could do a rousing rendition of the Italian folk song "Bella Ciao." I could play some simple spiritual songs on the guitar and get people to sing along.

So I announced that we would be having a RAWA evening. RAWA is an acronym for the Renaissance Artists and Writers Association. It is a department of Ananda Marga set up by Baba in 1958. The purpose of RAWA is to encourage artistic expression that raises spiritual and social consciousness and to free art from the shackles of political and commercial interests. RAWA activities include providing opportunities for artists to express themselves in specially arranged concerts, organizing artists' cooperatives, and recording and publishing material created in the spirit of "art for service and blessedness."

We didn't have a big network of contacts and friends to begin with, but I went ahead anyway and told the other monks and nuns in Tokyo about it and asked them to invite guests to our first evening "concert." Predictably only a few people came to that first RAWA evening, but I was persistent. I organized another evening a few weeks later and some more people came, but still my colleagues didn't take this enterprise very seriously. Then, I found a way to advertise our programs to an interested audience. There were some English language newspapers in Tokyo. *The Japan Times* was one of them. They had a free classified advertising section and I announced the next RAWA program in that newspaper. The newspaper was not only read by foreign English speakers but by Japanese people who wanted to improve their English language skills and try new things. This was just perfect for us.

The advertisements in *The Japan Times* brought some new faces to our RAWA programs and now all of my colleagues became enthusiastic. Dada Satyaparananda, in particular, jumped into action. He started cooking sumptuous Indian vegetarian meals that were served at the conclusion of the music portion of the program and also gave short talks about meditation, which were included as part of the program.

Now we had a basic formula that worked. We would advertise the programs in the newspaper and when people arrived they would become part of our mailing list. I would begin the program with a short introduction to RAWA and our concept of art. Then the various presenters would sing, recite poems, play musical instruments, and sometimes present works of visual art. Increasingly, the artists were not members of Ananda Marga. Somewhere in the middle of the program, Dada S would give his short talk, and at the end everyone sat around our tablecloth spread out on the tatami mats and enjoyed a meal.

With our full-moon festivals, we were able to make a lot of new friends and many of them learned meditation from us. The number of participants in our weekly meditation sessions began to grow, and when I was about to leave Tokyo in May of 1984, I counted more than thirty people at one of the Sunday meditation sessions. After I left Tokyo the RAWA evenings continued to grow.

Becoming an Avadhuta

In March of 1983 I was called to India to become *avadhuta*. This was a big thing. In my previous visits to India I had tried to become an avadhuta but without success. Now, instead of me clamoring to get the initiation, India was calling me.

I flew to Bangladesh on the national airline of that small country. When the plane landed in Dacca, everyone on the plane started clapping. I had never experienced anything like this before and wondered if the plane was so unsafe that the people had let out an exclamation of relief on landing. Later as I traveled around the world I found that in many developing countries, this is normal at the end of a flight.

Once again, due to the Indian blacklist, I was not able to get an Indian visa prior to my visit. I was hoping that I could find some way to cross over the border without having to pass through a normal checkpoint. I took a bus from Dacca to the border and arrived in a small town. I wandered around it and first tried to cross by myself but was unsuccessful. Then I went back to the town and eventually found some people who could take me across the border. This delayed my scheduled arrival in Calcutta but it worked. They took me into the forest, where we waited in a small hamlet consisting of a few mud houses. Later they took me out again and I walked a short distance till I reached a road on the Indian side of the border. All of a sudden a bicycle rickshaw appeared on the road and told me to get in. He handed me a note written by a margi and then took me to the home of that margi, who ran an Ananda Marga school.

I was amazed by this. I had wandered across the border with no idea of where I was or where I was going and all of a sudden I was being taken to the home of a margi. Later I asked that margi how he knew I was coming and how everything had been arranged. All he said was, "a rickshaw driver told me."

From there I boarded a train for Calcutta. After my arrival, I was walking on the street when someone hit me in the back with a water balloon filled with colored water. It was the full moon of March, the day when the Indian color festival, *Holi*, is celebrated. Throwing colored powder and sometimes colored water at people is part of the festival. I didn't know what was going on at the time, however. I just wanted to get to Baba's house as soon as possible.

When I reached Baba's residence at Lake Gardens, the person in charge of arranging the avadhuta initiations saw me and seemed relieved that I had finally arrived. He embraced me and said that Baba had inexplicably delayed giving the initiations till now.

I waited with the other monks who were selected for this initiation and finally we went into a room where Baba taught us *kapalika* meditation. *Kapalika* means "the one who protects the created universe." It is a special meditation that tantric adepts perform once a month at the time of the new moon. The meditation is practiced outdoors in a cremation grounds, cemetery, or a lonely place, and one of its goals is to overcome fear, shyness, shame, and other mental propensities. This meditation dates back to the time of Shiva, approximately 5000 BCE. While Baba was explaining the process, he demonstrated something using his hand and then quipped, "Did they have hands seven thousand years ago?"

When the instruction was completed, I took an oath and was given a new name. I was now Vedaprajinananda Avadhuta. *Veda* means knowledge and *Prajina* (pronounced "prag-ya") literally means "perfect knowing" or "perfect knowledge" and is commonly understood as "wisdom". So the name Vedaprajinananda can be translated as "the one who attains bliss (*ananda*) through knowledge and wisdom." I now adopted the full orange dress, whereas before I wore an orange gown and white trousers.

Following my initiation as an avadhuta, I returned to Japan and continued my work there.

On the Road in Japan

While I was in Tokyo, I missed the adventures I used to have in France. In France I rarely stayed in my office and would spend most of the month touring various cities. That's why I jumped at a chance to get out of Tokyo to visit margis in other places.

We had some contacts in the city of Sapporo, which is on the northern island of Hokkaido, and I arranged a visit there, deciding to travel by a combination of hitchhiking, bullet train, and boat. On the way I also planned to stop in the homes of some people who were interested in learning meditation.

When I had started touring in France, five years earlier, one of the first things that I did was learn a few French words and phrases—specifically, I learned the necessary vocabulary for teaching the basic meditation lesson. I did this by getting my French friends to make a small booklet that contained the meditation lesson instructions. Based on that experience, I asked the dada who was fluent in Japanese to prepare a booklet for me with the basic vocabulary I would need. When it was done, I studied it and put it into my backpack.

As per the plan, I started off the trip by hitching a ride on the roads outside Tokyo. At one point I also got on a train and continued north. Before I reached the northern limit of Honshu Island (the main island on which Tokyo is located) I decided to visit a place where I had the address of a boy who had expressed interest in learning meditation. Despite the great difficulty caused by my limited Japanese vocabulary, I was able to locate the house. As was the case with some of my early experiences in France, neither of us was very proficient in the other's language. Somehow we managed to communicate and with the help of my booklet I taught him meditation. I am not sure how much he really absorbed but between this teaching experience and the effort to find the way to his home, my ability to converse in Japanese was growing.

After this short visit, I continued on my way and soon reached the northern port city of Aomori, where there was a overnight ferry to Hokkaido. I boarded the ferry and arrived in the port across the strait early in the morning, around 5:00 AM. There was no train connection to Sapporo for several hours and as I sat in the terminal building, I was wondering what to do, asking Baba to help me utilize the time for something worthwhile.

As I was thinking this, one of the workers in the terminal came over and asked me what I was doing. He thought I looked a little lost and asked if he should call the police to help me out. I said no and then told him that I was a yoga teacher. Then he thumbed through a directory and made a phone call. I was skeptical, doubting that anything would come of it so early in the morning, but after he finished his call he came over to me and told me that someone would be coming to pick me up. It turned out to be a woman yoga teacher. Her husband was a doctor who ran a small clinic attached to their residence.

The woman, who was very well off and able to spend a lot of her time teaching yoga, kept me busy from morning to night. I taught at some of her yoga classes, introduced the Baba Nam Kevalam mantra for chanting and meditation, and between yoga classes groups of young Japanese students came by to converse with me in the hope of improving their English-language skills. At one point a newspaper crew came and interviewed me and later did a story about my visit. I had mentally asked Baba to make my short stay in the city of Hakodate worthwhile and he more than fulfilled my request.

The next day I headed on to Sapporo where I met some margis and held a group meditation session with them. Sapporo was covered with snow and I saw remnants of the ice sculptures that had been made for a famous annual winter festival in the city.

After my visit to Sapporo, I went back to Tokyo, feeling that with a few more trips like that I would really be able to learn Japanese.

Back to Europe

Just as I was starting to get adjusted to Japan and beginning to learn Japanese, however, I received word that I had been transferred again. I was being sent back to Europe to serve as the sectorial office secretary for Berlin Sector.

I had already served as the Regional Secretary in France, but now I was to work in the office that coordinated Ananda Marga work throughout Europe. I was not so enthusiastic about the transfer because in Tokyo we really had a great "esprit de corps." Selling paintings in the evening was hard, but we were all doing it together for a common cause. The RAWA programs were inspiring and we were starting to teach meditation to more and more people in Japan. So I didn't hurry back to Europe and instead continued to work in Tokyo for a few months more.

Our Ananda Marga office in Europe was located in the city of Mainz. Finally in May of 1984 the pressure to reach there became too much to resist and I boarded the long flight from Tokyo to Frankfurt. Although Baba had designated Berlin as the headquarters for Ananda Marga in Europe, we found it easier to work in this medium-sized city near Frankfurt. One of the reasons for this was that West Berlin at the time was an island in the middle of communist East Germany. To get there you had to drive slowly through East Germany on a heavily guarded road. It was kind of creepy and also inconvenient because at that time most Ananda Marga work was taking place in Western Europe.

My job in Mainz was much more difficult than my job in Tokyo because Ananda Marga was active in more countries in Berlin Sector and the administrative work was more complex. The finances were more complicated as well. We had a huge office and a lot of bills to pay but we did not have a fixed or steady income. At one point I even decided to import some paintings from Hong Kong and went to some flea markets to sell them.

I was working in Mainz for about a year when one day the monk in charge of the sector came back from India and informed us that we had to move our office to Berlin. He explained that during the meeting in India that he had just attended, some of the monks working in Africa had tried to get permission to move their office from Nairobi to a city in Zambia. Baba explained that he had chosen the sectorial headquarters with careful deliberation and they shouldn't be changed. The location of our office in Europe had already been changed several years back but our sectorial secretary wanted to correct the change. "You have to go to Berlin, computer and all," he told me, so I packed up as much office equipment as I could and "moved the office" to West Berlin, to an apartment that we were renting as the local headquarters.

I moved, but the office really didn't move, because Berlin was still inconveniently located in the middle of East Germany. When people had to travel to India or other places in the sector, the nearby Frankfurt airport made Mainz the logical choice rather than Berlin. When we called monks and nuns for the bi-monthly reporting sessions, Mainz was also more convenient, both for ease of travel and because we had a much larger building there. As a result, I had to commute often between Mainz in West Germany and Berlin in East Germany.

Berlin and the Iron Curtain

The atmosphere in Berlin was quite different than that of West Germany. There was more evidence of avant-garde, radical, and punk culture. West Berlin was a varied, lively and cosmopolitan city. One day I was out walking when all of a sudden I came upon a white wall covered with all kinds of colorful paintings, murals, and graffiti. It turned out to be the fearsome Berlin Wall that the communists had erected in 1961, dividing the two parts of Berlin in order to keep their population from fleeing to West Germany.

I was curious to know what lay on the other side of that wall, especially knowing that Baba had instructed us to spread our ideas in Eastern Europe. It was possible to visit East Berlin but it was an intimidating experience. You had to go to one of the designated crossing points. The most famous one was Checkpoint Charlie, home to a well-known museum commemorating the attempts by East German citizens to cross the walls and barbed wire to seek asylum in West Germany.

One Saturday afternoon I went to one of the crossing points. I had to pass a number of officers who checked my passport with great attention. They had a machine that emanated a spooky blue light in which they put the passport. They also searched my pockets for leaflets or other contraband. I then had to change some "hard currency" (dollars or West German Marks) for their East German currency before I was able to walk through the gates into East Berlin. Although I was only a few hundred feet away from West Berlin, it seemed like I had passed into another world.

After that I visited East Berlin a number of times. Sometimes I went to coffee shops in the main shopping plaza at Alexander Platz. In the middle of this busy plaza was a giant tower that served as the main transmitting antenna for East German television. The observation deck and restaurant near the top of the structure was also one of East Berlin's biggest tourist attractions. In the coffee shops around the tower I met young people and told them about yoga and meditation but I did not have much chance to do anything more.

One time in East Berlin I attended the Festival of Political Song where I saw an American troupe called The Bread and Puppet Theater perform. The festival was held in a large convention center, and during an intermission period I sat in the lobby of the building and tried to do my midday meditation. One of the guards came up to me and nudged me with his stick. I guess meditation was not permitted there. I was wearing civil dress rather than my orange robes, but it seemed that meditating in public was not allowed in East Berlin.

I also used to cross in and out of East Germany on my commutes from Mainz to Berlin. Cars from West Germany would have to go to a large border area where the documents of both the car and passengers were checked under the "high-tech" East German fluorescent blue-light boxes. Then the cars would travel slowly (sixty mph was the top speed allowed) on a carefully watched highway with surveillance towers scattered along the route. Between the border station with its long wait and document check, and the tedious drive along the East German highway, it was quite a hassle.

I didn't own a car but I used to travel with ride-share services. One time in 1986 or 1987, I was in a car crossing East Germany on my way to West Berlin when I startled the owner by telling him that in our lifetime the Berlin Wall and this East German border would come down. He didn't believe me, of course, but my prediction came true a few short years later.

I was not clairvoyant but I had come to this conclusion due to a general belief that was widespread in Ananda Marga.

In 1955 Baba had reassured some disciples, telling them that he would be around for another fifty years and that during this period, the mission of establishing a world where spiritual values were honored would be completed. So I thought that by 2005 a lot of the major problems of the world would be "solved," and communism was certainly one of these problems. In his book *Human Society*, Baba also mentioned that the military rule of the communists had been challenged prematurely by intellectuals in Hungary in 1956 and would again be challenged afterwards.

I really believed that this would happen but thought that it would be after the year 2000. I was just as surprised as anyone else when communism in Eastern Europe began to collapse at the end of 1989, and in the years that followed I was able to visit all of the former communist countries of Eastern Europe.

Whirlwind Tour in Poland

Even before communism collapsed, we started to do some amazing work in Eastern Europe. One of the most active places for Ananda Marga in the late 1980s was Poland. Poland was a staunch Catholic country and it was not possible for the communists to stamp out religion or spirituality there. While Lech Walesa was leading the Solidarity labor movement against the communist government, the young people of Poland took a keen interest in many forms of Eastern spirituality. Teachers of all types were active in Poland—Zen, Hare Krishna and of course, Ananda Marga. We were allowed to work without much official obstruction, and some people even speculated that the communist government tolerated this New Age spirituality as a way to counter the influence of the Catholic Church, which they saw as one of their biggest enemies.

Whatever the explanation, in the late 1980s Poland was a great place to teach meditation. I began visiting Poland in 1987 and Ananda Marga already had a large following with centers in several cities. Some of the margis organized an action-packed tour of several cities. I didn't have a chance to rest for even a single minute. Even while walking in the Warsaw train station, margis came from nowhere to ask me to give them a spiritual name or answer questions about meditation. I was dressed in civil clothes during my travel around Poland but would change into my orange uniform at the site of my lectures and other programs. The margis who met me unexpectedly in the train station recognized me because I was walking with other meditators whom they knew well.

The Warsaw train station was big and bustling. With its high ceilings, large lobby area, and busy food and magazine vendors, it was not much different from the stations I had seen in other parts of Europe. The trains were also laid out similarly to the ones in Western Europe but the equipment was old, in sharp contrast to the train systems of France and Germany where it seemed like new carriages were introduced on a yearly basis.

My tour took me to Warsaw, Chojnow, Wroclaw, and Katowice, and I gave many lectures. The organization of some of these lectures was quite interesting. The margis arranged a room in a university and put up some posters only a few hours before the event; yet even so there was a full house. The thirst for new things was amazing. From such a short and rapid tour, I could not tell if there was much difference between the students in Poland and their Western counterparts, though when I later went on a slower-paced tour in Hungary I did observe one important difference: "We cheered when we heard that the Americans had bombed Hanoi," one man who had been a student in the 1960s told me in Budapest in 1990. I didn't tell him that many students in the US were not so happy about this event.

During that week-long tour in Poland, I gave personal instruction in meditation to more than one hundred people. In one instance I was giving a lecture to a packed audience, many of whom wanted to learn meditation, but I couldn't finish the lecture and teach the people meditation because I had to leave for an event in another city. Luckily, a nun was traveling with us and she was able to finish the lecture and at least teach meditation to the women in the audience.

This tour of Poland and other visits in the period just before the fall of the communists paved the way for Ananda Marga's purchase of large rural centers in 1990 and afterwards.

And the Winner is ....

During the late 1980s, I also spent a lot of time in Scandinavia. In fact, when I wasn't in Poland or in Germany I was either in Norway, Sweden,

Denmark, or Finland. By this time, Scandinavia and all of Western Europe had slowed down with regard to the acceptance of Ananda Marga. The late 1970s and first part of the 1980s were indeed the glory days, with many young people flocking to Ananda Marga, learning meditation, and joining the ranks of full-time volunteers. As the novelty of Eastern mysticism wore off, it became more difficult to draw people to our programs. Other factors may have also played a role, such as the changing political and economic climate in Europe and the world, but it is hard to pin it down to one specific thing.

Despite the slowdown, there were active Ananda Marga units in the major cities such as Oslo, Copenhagen, Stockholm, and Helsinki, and I visited all of these places. An interesting Ananda Marga center was set up near the medium-sized Swedish city of Örebro. Although the city dates back to the Middle Ages, its well-kept buildings and state-of-the-art infrastructure made it look as modern as could be. In an agricultural area just outside the city, margis from Norway and Sweden purchased a large country house that they divided into several apartments, setting up a housing cooperative and spiritual community, complete with a meditation hall and a small kindergarten.

The Ananda Marga lifestyle tends to attract similar people in the different countries I visited and so I felt at home wherever I went. The cultures and languages of Sweden and Norway are particularly close, and if you didn't know the people, it would be hard to tell who was from which country. One time I watched as a Norwegian friend spoke with a Swede. Afterward I asked him which language he was speaking. "He was speaking Swedish and I answered him in Norwegian," he told me.

The people often invited me for retreats and I enjoyed their warm company. One time during a retreat in Örebro we held a tandava competition and I was one of the judges. Tandava is a strenuous dance—I had heard that when Baba first introduced it he personally danced it for seventeen minutes. We used to determine the winners based on both their form and their stamina. About ten men took part in the Örebro competition. It doesn't last too long since it is really hard to keep jumping and raising your legs while keeping your arms extended horizontally. I watched them jump until only two were left, watching closely to see who kept the proper form. When the dancing stopped, I was ready to declare one the winner and the other the runner-up, when someone pointed to the back of the room. Still standing was Pavan, an eight-year-old boy who had kept pace with the grownups. I was not sure what to do, since I had not even seen the little boy dancing in the back, so I declared all three the winners.

Visiting India in the 1980s, Various Incidents

My life in Europe in this period was punctuated with yearly trips to India, ostensibly to give reports to Baba. These meetings no doubt had significance to our organization because they enabled Ananda Marga to grow and develop around the world in a uniform way. But I also believe that they had more than just an organizational significance, since they enabled us to be close to Baba.

These were intimate experiences, normally around twenty or thirty acharyas and Baba. During the New Year and in June, when Ananda Marga held its bi-annual big gatherings, the number of monks and nuns in these meetings would get much larger.

I was fortunate to be in some of the smaller meetings where I got a chance to see the various sides of Baba: Baba, the stern administrator; Baba, the humorist; Baba, the walking encyclopedia.

One time I was in a meeting with some acharyas. Baba was taking a report from Dada Pranavananda, who was the publications secretary at that time. The deadline for printing one of Baba's books had come and Baba wanted to know if the book was ready. He questioned Dada P, and Dada became uneasy because the book was not ready and Baba seemed to be in a fierce mood. Baba asked Dada if he had indeed declared that the book would be ready today. Dada squirmed and then said that the target date that he had declared was actually a "slip of the tongue or a slip of the pen," and that it wasn't really supposed to be ready now. He braced himself for a rebuke from Baba, who usually didn't like to hear excuses. But instead of a rebuke, Baba started to tell a story.

Once there was a lawyer, he said, who had a reputation for efficiency and punctuality. However, this lawyer missed an important date in court, failing to show up to represent his client. When he finally showed up in the courtroom a few days later, the judge questioned him about his absence. "I could not reach the court on that day," the lawyer explained, "because there was a 'play-gwee' in my village."

The judge was puzzled by the lawyer's reply and then said out loud, "Play-gwee? Do you mean plague?"

The lawyer said, "Yes, that is what I meant."

The judge was still puzzled and said, "Sir, you are a learned lawyer and well versed in English (the language used in the courts of India). How could you make the mistake of pronouncing plague as 'play-gwee?'"

"Excuse me, your honor," the lawyer replied. "It was a slip of the ton-gwee."

The Walking Encyclopedia

When Baba was a youth and later when he started working in the accounts office of the Indian railways in Jamalpur, he was known as a "walking encyclopedia." He seemed to know everything about any subject from botany to physics to human history.

In addition to spiritual subjects, the books that Baba wrote as an adult include essays on linguistics, history, science, medicine, botany, political science, philosophy, psychology and many other subjects. As acharyas working in close proximity to Baba, we were often treated to displays of his knowledge in these fields.

On one of my yearly visits to India during the 1980s, there was a reporting session where Baba's encyclopedic knowledge was put on display. At that time Baba was taking reports from district secretaries from around the world. The various monks and nuns had the task of bringing the district secretaries to the meetings in Calcutta. During one evening session, a young woman representing the Jakarta district of Indonesia stepped forward. Baba asked her which district she represented. When she said, "Jakarta," Baba explained the meaning of the name. He pointed out that the word *jakarta* was originally Sanskrit, Sanskrit being spoken throughout large portions of South Asia in ancient times, and that it was derived from the words *jaya* and *karta*, which together mean "victory to the Lord."

Baba then asked her a long series of questions about the geography of her district, beginning with, "Is it in a volcanic belt?" The girl was unable to answer the questions but each time Baba himself supplied the answers, telling about the geography, climate, flora, and fauna of the area. I don't remember all the questions and answers, but I do remember that it was a dazzling display of knowledge. When Baba was leaving the hall, he stopped and turned to the general secretary. "GS Dada," he said, "and you thought that your Baba didn't know anything about geography?"

On another occasion I had the good fortune to be standing before Baba and answering—or attempting—to answer his questions. I say good fortune because I wanted Baba's attention even if it meant getting scolded for a deficient report or getting called out for conduct that was not up to the mark. I wanted to get his guidance, either harsh or sweet. This time it was sweet.

During in the 1980s, Baba wrote a book on English grammar and he also coined new words in Sanskrit as well. Whenever he issued new material, he liked to test the acharyas and margis who came before him in reporting sessions to see if they were up to date with his newest writings. During one evening meeting in Lake Gardens, Baba called on me to answer some questions. First he asked me, "What is the proper Sanskrit term for 'television?'" Of course there were no televisions around when Sanskrit was a living language, so a new term had to be invented for the modern era. The Indian government coined the term *doordarshan*, which combines two Sanskrit words that together mean "far seeing." Baba was not satisfied with the term because in television there is not only seeing but hearing as well. So he coined a new term, *shiitaka*, which means "seeing and hearing." I had heard about this, but when Baba questioned me all I could remember was *doordarshan*.

Then he started to ask about some English words. He asked me, "What is the meaning of draught." This is a tricky word; it can be pronounced liked "draft" and one meaning of it is to take a drink of water or other liquid. Baba helped me get the answer by making a movement with his hand as if he was drinking some water. Beer stored in kegs is often called "draught beer."

It is possibly for this reason that the next question was "What does 'dry movement' mean?" Baba had explained this in his book on grammar. I remembered his explanation and said that it referred to movements to prohibit the manufacture, sale, and consumption of alcoholic beverages. Baba said that my answer was correct. Then he started to tell an anecdote about the leader of a dry movement who gave a long speech about the evils of alcohol and then went home and celebrated his successful speech with an alcoholic drink. Baba once again brought his hand near his mouth, mimicking the movement of a drinker, and everyone laughed.

The next question got into more serious matters. The word was "drought." Baba asked me, "What are the causes of droughts?" I only knew part of the answer. I said that excessive deforestation changes climates and can bring diminished rainfall and drought.

Baba said that this was correct and then gave two more reasons. He said that the changing positions of low-pressure centers located in the oceans off continents is the second cause, and the third one is changes in the angular positions (in relation to the Earth) of certain stars and other celestial bodies. He said that at present humans only had control over the first cause of drought, but that in the future advances in meteorological and marine sciences will allow humans to be able to do something about the second cause. Regarding the angular positions of celestial bodies, he said that this was only in the jurisdiction of the Supreme Consciousness.

After he said this, I sat down, thoroughly satisfied with this session. Later the information that he gave on the causes of drought in that reporting session were incorporated in a formal essay called "Water Conservation," published on March 25, 1989.

The "Terrifying" World Review

In 1985 we received word that Baba was conducting a "World Review." This was something new and unique, and I was required to go to India to take part in it.

Normally each month, representatives from different parts of the world came to India and gave their reports in front of Baba and the central administration, but now Baba was calling batches of whole-time workers (monks and nuns) to come to India so that he could review their work. The batches were arranged according to particular work designations. For example at that time I was the office secretary for Berlin Sector, so I had to present myself in front of Baba along with all the other office secretaries from around the world. It was still impossible for known margis to get visas to India, so I bought a ticket to Bangladesh and traveled by land to Calcutta.

The World Review meetings took place at Baba's house in Lake Gardens. Baba was in a very strict mood and he was not at all satisfied with anyone's work. Finally he told all of us, the seven or eight office secretaries from around the world, that we were no longer monks and we should leave his house immediately!

As shocking as this sounded, it was routine for the World Review. The same thing had already happened to other batches of monks that had given their reports to Baba. The central-level monks gave us instructions. We were to leave Baba's house and change into civil dress. Then we were to wait across the street from the house. At the proper time, we could then make an appeal to Baba to reconsider our status.

So we went across the street and watched Baba's comings and goings and the other events taking place in the front courtyard of the house. I was sure Baba wasn't so disgusted with us that he never wanted to see us again, and this was confirmed after a day or two.

It was Sunday, time for the weekly dharmachakra (collective meditation). The weekly collective meditation is the most important social and spiritual function in Ananda Marga. Members are supposed to meditate twice a day, and once a week they should attend collective meditation.

So that Sunday, we defrocked and expelled office secretaries requested that we be allowed to attend the collective meditation program that afternoon. The request was sent to Baba and after some deliberation he said, "They have performed yeoman service for humanity. Let them attend." The word "yeoman" in this context means "one who performs great and loyal service." So really, in Baba's eyes we were not such bad fellows after all.

A few days later as the World Review was coming to an end, we were reinstated and asked to come to Baba's house. I am well aware that this scenario may seem odd or irrational to someone on the outside but I believe that Baba used this kind of drama to make us realize that he expected great work from us, that we shouldn't get complacent or think that we knew everything or that we were exalted just because we were wearing orange robes.

Another possible explanation for the World Review is that once again it was an opportunity for the disciples to be with the guru. Had the World Review not been called, we would have not gone to India. Baba wanted to see us and he wanted us to be with him. Thus the World Review was, in a way, a convenient excuse. In any case, I remember the closing session of the World Review in which the general secretary announced that the "terrifying World Review is now over."

The World Review was dramatic, but the drama didn't end for me and another monk, Dada Rudreshvarananda. We still had to go over land from Calcutta to Dacca in Bangladesh. It wasn't a long trip, but because we had come to India on such short notice and without proper visas, we had to somehow leave India without going through a normal border checkpoint.

We went to a small village on the India–Bangladesh border. There one margi arranged for a boatman to take us across the river that separated the two countries. Somewhere around midnight he took us across the fields to the riverbank, but we could not carry out the plan. The area was crawling with border police who were looking for some smugglers. When we saw the police, we ducked into the brush and waited. Though the police shined their searchlights all around and actually came quite close to us, they did not see us.

We ended up hiding there for a long time. While we were waiting, we could hear the chanting of the Hare Krishna mantra coming from a nearby village. It sounded like the whole village was out there chanting. When we could no longer hear any other activity in the area we left our hiding place and walked to the riverbank but there was no sign of the boat or the boatman. So we lifted our bags over our heads and waded out into the river. Fortunately it was very shallow at that particular place and we were able to traverse it without any great difficulty. Once we got on the other side, we were able to reach a place where there was bus service to Dacca.

Years later, in 2003, I was in the US for the summer and I met Dada Rudreshvarananda again. He looked at me and said, "We have not seen each other since the time we crossed the river into Bangladesh!" It was as if the incident in Bangladesh had just happened and suddenly we were together again. Dada R has passed on since then, departing from this world. Who knows? Maybe one day I will see him again in another incarnation, and we will once more feel that the barriers of time and space have been traversed in a flash.

Flooded in Tiljala

In September of 1986, I was in India representing Berlin Sector in the monthly reporting sessions. There were a lot of margis visiting India at this time and there was a festive atmosphere at our ashram in Tiljala, making our stay quite enjoyable. In the meantime, it kept raining and raining. Soon the water was unable to drain away and the ashram was covered with a foot of water. Despite this, our spirits were not dampened. We waded happily through the water to get from the main ashram building to Baba's residence, which was situated behind it. Still the water kept rising. We saw people wading through the water with their clothes on their heads to keep them dry. The water kept on rising and at one point some devotees got into a small boat to cover the short distance to Baba's house. There were too many devotees in the boat, however, and it sunk. Still everyone seemed to be enjoying themselves.

Gradually, however, the flood became a serious problem for the thousands of people who lived in the area surrounding our compound. We started to realize the seriousness of the problem when we ran out of food supplies and heard that Baba had started fasting in solidarity with suffering people all around us.

Finally the conditions became so bad that Baba had to be taken out of the compound in a small boat. I stood on the top of the roof of the five-story building and watched as Baba got into the boat surrounding by swimming yogis. The boat made its way from the guru's residence through the compound's gate and into the street, which was now a waterway, not a road. Baba sat quietly in the boat while some monks paddled. The monks in the water were his honor guard. Baba's boat reached the higher ground of a nearby highway and he climbed aboard a bus that carried him to a part of the city that was not flooded.

The monks and nuns immediately formed a relief corps under the banner of the Ananda Marga Universal Relief Team and began helping the flooded residents, evacuating them by boat from their precarious residences and providing emergency food supplies. I met Dada Ramananda at the nearby highway where he was distributing food to a long line of waiting people, completely absorbed in his work. I asked him, "Dada, how are you going to do your meditation when you have so many people to look after?" "In this kind of situation," he replied, "I have only to close my eyes for a few seconds and I get tremendous concentration."

The Mysteries of Microvita, Pizza, and Atlantis

During the month of January, 1987, I was on tour in Italy. The milder weather there was a relief from the cold of Germany where I was working at that time. When it came time to do my late-night outdoor kapalik meditation, it was actually a comfortable nineteen degrees Celsius (68 F) on the beach in Sicily where I was sitting. But it was not Italy's weather that stood out on the tour. Rather it was finding out that Baba, once again, had introduced a new dimension to Ananda Marga philosophy. I received an envelope in the mail that contained copies of Baba's latest discourses. On the last day of 1986 he had given a talk entitled "Microvitum, the Mysterious Emanation of Cosmic Factor."

When I read the discourse I was blown away! Baba boldly stated that life in this universe does not originate from combinations of carbon molecules but rather depends on mysterious particles that he labeled microvitum (singular) and microvita (plural). He said that these particles are living, that they travel throughout the universe, and that they straddle the line between mind and matter. (In the tantric philosophy, matter is said to be derived from mind, which then animates living structures.) He went on to say that the understanding of microvita will help humanity to revolutionize science—particularly biology, chemistry, and physics.

I wasn't expecting anything like this because the earlier books that I had read on Ananda Marga philosophy describing a cosmic cycle in which pure consciousness is transformed into this material world and then evolves back into pure consciousness seemed to be complete, explaining everything under the sun from the origin of planets and stars to the creation and evolution of life. But I soon was to find out that this new concept of microvita could unlock even more mysteries, some of which were quite mundane and others, out of this world.

While I was in Bologna, I got into a friendly argument with one of the margi brothers there. I asserted that the pizza in New York was the best in the world. New York pizza is held in high esteem by many people in the US, but my Italian friend took offense to this. After all, pizza was invented in Italy. It is a national dish that is sold everywhere in the country and which only really flourished in the US after World War II, when returning servicemen created a demand for the product that they had first tasted in Italy. I guess he had never heard of the pizzeria in Tampa that imports water from New York so that it can get the "special something" of New York pizza in its Florida-made product.

My Italian friend didn't want to just argue about it; he made a direct challenge. He took me out to a pizzeria to prove his point. The restaurant was modern and well lit, but I was not going to prejudge the pizza based on the appearance of the restaurant. Back in the US, I had tasted great pizzas made in the most unlikely places. We ordered a big pizza and started eating. I was not impressed but I didn't say anything. It was not a particularly good pizza. Midway through the meal my friend said, "OK, I concede, New York pizza is better!" It is good that he gave up there and then so that we didn't have to try to figure out how to get to New York for the second round of the competition.

Only later, when I started to read more about microvita, could I understand why New York pizza is so prized that a pizzeria in Tampa went to the trouble of importing water from New York. Perhaps this new theory could explain why something prepared with exactly the same ingredients could produce a different taste in another place. In subsequent talks, Baba stated that the difference in the number and kinds of microvita that are contained in compounds can yield different outcomes. He gave the example of some munitions made from nitrates that turn out to be duds while other munitions made with the same mineral compounds from another area have high explosive power. After reading this, I thought that perhaps the presence of some special microvita in New York's water was the reason why I won the great pizza challenge in Bologna!

As I read the discourse on microvita, I was also struck by what this new theory had to say about psychological and spiritual matters. In the psychic realm, positive microvita are said to help inspire people to do great things, while negative microvita can induce destructive thoughts, leading to depression and suicide. Negative microvita can even have a collective impact on the whole society. Baba also said that depraved behavior attracts negative microvita.

A few years later I was present at a reporting session at Baba's Lake Gardens residence in Calcutta in which he elaborated on the impact of microvita on society. He was in the midst of asking us questions on various spiritual and social topics, when he asked, "Can anyone here, using the archaeology of earth or of any other planet, give an example of the collective influence of negative microvita?"

One dada answered, "Yes, Baba. The city of Pompeii had a decadent lifestyle and it was eventually destroyed by a volcano."

Baba then addressed that same monk and said, "And what is your opinion about Atlantis?"

The monk answered, "Atlantis had a civilization with developed science and they were misusing that science; as a consequence they were destroyed by a flood."

Baba didn't say directly if the answers were right or wrong. Rather he said, "It appears that this boy's guesses are correct."

Birds for Baba

When we started bringing plants to India for Baba's garden program, someone joked that next Baba would have us bringing animals as well. After all, neohumanism enjoins us to care for plants and animals and even inanimate objects. That joke turned into a reality when we received notice that we had to bring birds for aviaries that Baba was starting in Calcutta and Ananda Nagar. Whoever went to India for the monthly reporting sessions also had to bring a bird! It was challenging enough to bring plants, and sometimes great quantities of plants, to India but bringing a bird seemed even more difficult.

My turn to go to India came up again and the bird program was in full swing. There was no way around it. I would have to buy a bird and take it with me on the flight to India and the long train ride to Calcutta.

I went to a pet shop in Mainz and looked around until I selected a bird. I do not remember the exact species but it was a bird that normally spent a lot of time hopping around on the ground in search of food. By nature it was not a high flyer, but it would soon have to fly with me to India.

I put it in a cardboard box about the size of a shoebox and poked some holes in the box so that it could breathe. It was not an ideal arrangement, but it was the best I could do. When I passed through security at Frankfurt airport, the lady officer lifted the lid of my box and peaked in. She was charmed by the little bird and smiled.

On the airplane the bird sometimes jumped up and hit the top of the cardboard box but she managed to make it through the long flight without any real problems. I flew into Delhi and then boarded a train for the long journey to Calcutta. The crowded train ride was uncomfortable for me, and I imagine it was equally uncomfortable for my bird, confined in her little box. However, the hardest part of the journey was yet to come. At the bustling Howrah train station in Calcutta I met a bunch of orange-clad Ananda Marga monks. We decided to take a taxi together to our ashram in Tiljala, which was then on the outskirts of metropolitan Calcutta. In India it is not unusual to cram as many people as you can into a taxi. The dadas, who were usually very thin and very poor, had an extraordinary capacity to pack themselves into a taxi. I used to wonder if they didn't use a special yoga *mudra* to accomplish the task.

Our taxi, like all the others at that time, was an old Ambassador. The Ambassador was manufactured by Hindustan Motors of India. It was based on a British car of the late 1950s and Hindustan Motors continued to produce these cars with few improvements right up until 2014. Although the car was based on a 1950s model, to my eye it looked like something from the 1940s.

Three dadas crammed into the front with the driver and the rest of us were in the back. Our luggage was put in the trunk, but it couldn't close completely so the driver tied a rope from the trunk handle to the bumper, which somehow secured it all. I was seated in the back with the box carrying my bird on my lap. Among the monks who shared the back seat with me was a dada carrying a cage with two large green parrots. Leaving the train station, we crossed Howrah Bridge, a cantilever bridge with a suspended span over the Hooghly River. This is one of the busiest bridges in the world, carrying more than 100,000 vehicles per day and about 150,000 pedestrians. All manner of vehicles use the bridge, including large trucks and buses as well as taxis, private cars, and even pushcarts stacked high with all kinds of goods, all of them constantly tooting their horns in the Indian fashion, sometimes passing vehicles by going into the lane of oncoming traffic with their horn going full blast, warning everyone to stay clear.

The crowded bridge with its unrelenting cacophony really freaked out my little bird. She was hopping about in the cardboard box, hitting her head against the top. I glanced over at the monk carrying the birdcage with the two parrots. It was tilted because that was the only way we could fit it in the back, and I was amazed to see the birds chatting away happily, fully at home in an overcrowded car on India's busiest bridge.

Both my bird and I were happy when the taxi ride was over and we reached our headquarters in Tiljala. I deposited the bird with the monk in charge of this program and a few days later I saw it in a large enclosure along with several other birds. Sometime later, these birds were joined by two ostriches that were specially flown in from South Africa.

The Great Depression of 1990

In the late 1980s, the social philosophy of Ananda Marga was briefly thrust into the limelight due to the work of a margi economist, Dr. Ravi Batra, whose book *The Great Depression of 1990* became a worldwide bestseller. My colleagues and I saw this as an opportunity to reach a wider public, so we started to organize activities publicizing the book and the ideas behind it.

Dr. Batra, a professor of economics at Southern Methodist University in Dallas, argued that a study of the business cycle in the US pointed to the possibility of a sharp downturn in the year 1990. He also said that just prior to the stock market crash of 1929, wealth had become highly concentrated in the US and that now, in the late 1980s, the same levels of wealth concentration were being approached, a sign of a coming collapse. But what most intrigued me was when Batra, an ananda margi since his student days in India in the 1960s, elucidated his thesis by using Baba's concept of the social cycle. Batra said that the coming depression would not be just a typical economic downturn but would be part of events that would usher in a new era for humanity.

I received some of the early editions of the book, which Batra self-published, and I liked what I saw. Unlike most economists, Batra wrote in a lucid manner and his points were easily understood. He also had a knack for public speaking and his appearances on many radio talk shows enabled him to sell enough books to catch the interest of a major publisher, Simon & Schuster, which soon put out an edition that went to the number two position on the bestseller list.

Because Batra mentioned P.R. Sarkar and the book *Human Society Part II*, citing it as the source of his interest in the social cycle, we started to get attention from unforeseen places. One day I was in our headquarters in Mainz when I learned that someone from the embassy of Qatar had called up asking us to send them a copy of *Human Society II* as soon as possible.

Back in 1971 I had displayed copies of *Human Society II* in our Santa Monica jagriti. When my acharya saw this, he said, "That's a very revolutionary book." His tone of voice suggested that he questioned the wisdom of displaying it so openly. "Don't worry, Dada" I replied. "Very few people will be able to get past the first nine pages." Perhaps I should have said that very few people will get past the first sentence, which reads, "The existence of the relative factors of time, space and person is substantiated in the field of cognition, and the cognizant bearing in its inertness is the highest stance of these factors." From there Baba goes on to talk in an abstract fashion about the wave-like motion that is found both in nature and in the movement of society. Difficult or not, this book was now in demand and we seized the opportunity.

I was touring in France and Spain when I was dazzled by Ravi Batra's rise to fame. In Paris my former LFT volunteer Ramakrishna, who was now married, organized a public lecture in which I spoke about the social cycle and about Ravi Batra's book. This took place in the first week of September, 1987. On September 17, the stock market crashed and it seemed like Ravi Batra's prediction was coming true. I later learned that in the US, Batra was so inundated with phone calls that he recorded a message on his answering machine that said: "This is not it."

In Paris we were not sure if this was the start of the depression or not, but we did get excited. "Let's go to the university and talk with some economics professors," Ramakrishna said. We didn't know exactly what we were going to do, but we hurried to one of the University of Paris's campuses on the outskirts of the sprawling metropolis. Once we were there, Ramakrishna made a few inquiries and before we knew it we were thrust into a large classroom where an economics professor was giving a lecture. "We were just speaking about the Wall Street Crash and now you have come," he said to us. On the spot he turned over the class of some fifty students to me, and there I was, giving a lecture about the social cycle with my rusty French that I had picked up a decade early. Rusty or not, they liked the presentation and wanted to know more about the social cycle and Prout. A few days later I was walking on a Paris street when one of the people who had attended the lecture I had given at the beginning of the month came up to me and said, "You were right!"

For a while we rode this wave of interest. In western France one of the margis took me to newspaper office in Rennes, where I was interviewed for an article that appeared shortly thereafter. I also visited a newspaper office in Valencia where the interviewer took a keen interest in Batra's book and also in Prout. "How many Proutistas are there in Spain?" the journalist asked.

Now I was on the spot. I think he believed that we had a huge movement in Spain at that time. In reality we only had a handful of people but I did not want to disappoint him so I lifted my hands and arms and spread them out suggesting a large and wide following while remaining deliberately vague.

Some years later, Ananda Marga was battered by anti-sect articles in newspapers across Europe. These articles were usually instigated by various churches that did not want young people to join new religious movements. Sure enough, a newspaper in Valencia wrote a scathing article attacking Ananda Marga, warning the public that they had discovered five followers in Valencia.

The Great Depression did not come in 1990 but for a moment, at least, our ideas were being discussed on big public stage. Later in India, I learned that Baba had said, "The Cosmic Magician is behind the success of Ravi Batra." When I met Ravi in Finland, where he was promoting an edition of his book in Finnish, I told him what Baba had said and he lit up with a big smile.

New Renaissance Magazine, in Print and Online

Wherever I went in my travels with Ananda Marga, I always started some kind of newsletter or other printed journal. In my first assignment in Los Angeles, it was a newsletter that grew into the *Sadvipra* newspaper, which later became *The Universal Times*. When I went to France I edited a newsletter that was translated by my helpers and published in French. In Hong Kong I made a small newsletter for the PCAP, the ecological department of Ananda Marga. Later on, I also edited and published the newsletter for Ananda Marga in the Far East.

You could say that by this time writing and editing was in my blood. It was something I would do wherever you put me. Yogis would explain it by saying that it was my "samskara," the result of my past karma, which created a momentum that needed to be fulfilled in this way. This was my way of spending my time and in Europe I was again destined to get engaged in a major publishing effort.

During the 1980s my supervisor in Europe was Dada Shambhushivananda. Dada had a PhD in economics and had been a college professor before becoming an *acharya* of Ananda Marga. He encouraged me to make a small newsletter for the intellectual branch of Ananda Marga, which is known as Renaissance Universal or RU. When I was publishing *Sadvipra* and *The Universal Times* in the US, some of my margi friends published the *Renaissance Universal Journal*, a magazine on intellectual topics. Similarly, during the early 1980s, margis in England published a full-fledged magazine called *New Renaissance*. That magazine had been discontinued, so Dada suggested that I continue the tradition and call my journal *New Renaissance*.

During the mid-1980s I published a few issues of *New Renaissance* but it was a photocopied newsletter produced in limited quantities. It was not a printed magazine like the ones in the US and UK, so I really did not consider it to be "the real thing." However, sometime around 1988 we installed a small printing press in our Mainz office. By this time we were also using computers with the early versions of desktop publishing programs. In my days editing *Sadvipra* and *The Universal Times*, we had to do everything by hand. It was hard work. Now the tedious layout process could be done with a computer and a laser printer. The new programs produced columns with proportional type fonts, allowing us to do the whole layout on the computer screen. The laser-printed pages were then photographed and turned into plates, or alternatively the computer discs were given to the printers, who made plates directly from the digital information on the discs.

In December of 1989, the same month that the Berlin Wall began to come down, we produced our first copy of the revived *New Renaissance*. It was printed on our small printing press and sent throughout Europe and to other parts of the world as well. The magazine contained articles on ecology, politics, science, spirituality, and culture. There were book and music reviews as well.

Although the new computer programs made it easier to produce a magazine than it was in the days of cutting and pasting physical type rolls, it was by no means easy. There was also a long learning curve getting used to the computer. Sometime in the early 1990s, we were laying out an issue of *New Renaissance*. I was working with Dada Arjuna, my artistic layout guy. We had been working for several hours and had completed laying out around twenty pages of a thirty-six page magazine. All of a sudden the computer screen went black. Arjuna had accidentally disconnected the plug when his stretched foot under the desk hit the power cord. When the power was restored, we found that we had lost those twenty pages, having forgotten to save them as we went along!

Computer composition meant that we could do more elaborate types of magazine design, but in the end it seemed like we spent the same amount of time as we had when we had done the work by hand—it was still laborious.

While the first issues of the magazine were printed on our own press, as our activities in Poland increased, we found that we could take our computer discs to a printer in Poland and publish the magazine there. The printers in Poland provided us with full-color covers in a more professional format than was possible on our press, so I started taking the files to Poland. Later in the month, I would return to pick up the magazines and bring them back to Germany, where we would send them out to subscribers around the world.

Since the magazine was in English, I paid special attention to its distribution in England and often went there to promote it. Several bookshops in London used to sell the magazine, and we had a subscription drive in the UK with inserts and advertisements in magazines such as *The Ecologist* and *Resurgence*. Despite all these efforts, however, we were never able to reach a large audience. We did not have the budget to do the advertising needed to increase our circulation significantly, and being based in Germany when our biggest potential markets were in the UK and the US only compounded the problem.

Technology came to our rescue around 1995. Arun, a margi from Finland, approached me at the summer retreat in Germany. He had a digital camera and offered to take photos of the covers and put the magazine on the Internet. By this time I had used email and had a vague idea of the Internet, though I had never used a browser to surf websites.

I gave Arun some back issues along with the files for the latest issue, and an Internet version of the magazine appeared on the web in late 1995. In the months that followed, I became an avid Internet surfer and began to help edit the online edition as well as the printed edition. I published all the articles from the back issues online and in the years to come our website located at www.ru.org began to attract a relatively large volume of Internet visitors. When we had a printed journal, we were only able to print and distribute around 1000–1500 copies four times a year. This meant that at most 18,000 people per year had contact with our magazine (four issues x 1500 copies x three readers per copy equals 18,000). And that 18,000 figure is generous because many copies of the magazine were not distributed properly. Today, due to the power of the Internet, *New Renaissance* magazine gets more than ten thousand visitors every month.

I continued editing the magazine until 1998. Some of the highlights included interviews with economic activist David Korten and with Donovan, the singer-songwriter from the hippie era. In 1998 I went to my next assignment in the Middle East and the Balkans. My colleague and friend, Dada Jyotirupananda, continued publishing the print version of *New Renaissance* till 2005. Today, like many formerly printed journals, it continues only as an Internet publication.

7

Baba Moves On

*D*URING THE LATTER part of the 1980s, I was able to go to India every year because I was a department secretary and once a year each department secretary had to go to India to take part in one of the monthly reporting sessions with Baba. My final visit of the decade was in October 1989. During that year Baba put a lot of emphasis on the "master unit" program. Master unit is the name that Baba gave to the rural social service and education centers that Ananda Marga was setting up around the world. They were conceived as central hubs designed to invigorate the economy and culture of the surrounding region.

The first master unit was Ananda Nagar in West Bengal. When Ananda Nagar was first established, the adjacent village, Pundag, was a sleepy hamlet on the railroad line. Today it is a bustling town with all kinds of economic activities. Ananda Nagar, which was once a treeless desert, is now a verdant campus with educational institutions ranging from preschools to a degree college.

During the October, 1989, reporting sessions, Baba spoke about master units. In the concluding meeting, just before the representatives returned to their respective sectors, he said with great solemnity, "These master units will become cultural centers, places from where we can popularize our ideology."

Those were the last words that I was to hear from Baba. I was not able to go to India for reporting the following year because Baba called the directors of the various master units. They became the representatives for their respective sectors instead of the department secretaries.

Poland Master Unit

Back in Europe, we also caught the master unit bug. We tried to buy land in several different countries, including Poland. While I was on tour in Poland in 1990, one of my supervisors, Dada Artapremananda, called me on the phone and said that we should find some land there that we could develop into a master unit.

I was in the southwest of the country at the time, visiting margis. We looked in the immediate area and did in fact find a piece of land with a small farmhouse. I called Dada and told him we had found some land for the master unit, but when I told him how small it was, he said that we should continue looking, giving preference to the areas near the German border. I went with Rameshvar to several places but we couldn't find anything that seemed suitable. I felt defeated by the circumstances, but just at that moment, as we were seated in Rameshvar's house in Chojnow in the Silesian region of southwest Poland, a margi stopped by to tell us that he knew of an eighty-hectare farm that someone was selling, more than large enough for a master unit. It was located only twenty minutes away from the city of Jelenia Gora.

We went there immediately. It turned out to be thirty-two hectares, not eighty, but it was bigger than anything we had seen up until that point. Not only was it big, it was beautiful, a dairy farm nestled in a valley overlooked by Mount Schneekoppe, or Sněžka in Polish, which means "snow-capped," exactly what the mountain is. The location was beautiful and it had land that could be cultivated as well as used as pasture land. The present owner was not a typical farmer but a city dweller who had gone back to the land to farm. He had contracted cancer and could not work the land anymore, thus he had put it up for sale.

Scene at the master unit in Poland. Our land is in the foreground. Mt. Sněžka is the highest peak on the ridge with a small structure barely visible at the top.

I sat with Rameshvar and Mahaviira and, as we talked to the man, I wondered whether we could handle such a huge responsibility. But we went ahead and told him we would purchase it. This was in the spring of 1990 and Poland had just been liberated from communist rule. Land prices were low compared to Western Europe, much lower than they are today in Poland. The price was low but to a monk, it seemed like a lot.

I had margi friends in Norway, Sweden, Germany, Italy, and other countries of Western Europe. With their generous donations, we were able to make the down payment. We got an old farmhouse on thirty hectares, one Russian tractor and seventeen cows for less than twenty thousand dollars. But I was unable raise all the money we needed. Three thousand dollars still remained to be paid and I was not sure how I would get it. I told the farmer that I would pay the remainder later in the summer, after I returned from an ecological festival in Hungary, but I had no real idea how I would raise the money, since the festival would only be attended by young people and hippies!

I put the problem in the back of my mind and went to Ecotopia, a camping festival organized by a Holland-based organization called European Youth Forest Action. They held the festival each summer in a different location. Now that the Iron Curtain had fallen, they seized on the opportunity to hold their festival in Hungary. During the festival there were workshops on sustainability, agriculture, spirituality, and other themes. I gave a meditation workshop. But my problem of returning to Poland with the necessary payment did not go away.

On the last day of the festival, I attended a workshop on project development and fundraising. The leader of the workshop, Wam Kat from the Netherlands, asked each participant to explain his or her project. I explained that we had just purchased a farm in Poland but needed a bit more to make the final payment (which was actually to cover the cost of the tractor and the cows). When the workshop was over, Wam Kat approached me and said, "A lot of Polish people came to this festival and they paid us in Polish money. We can't use it in Holland and we have a whole pile of it."

He counted out the money. It was exactly the amount I needed to make the final payment. "I can give this money to you as a loan," he said, "and you can send me reports on the progress of the project and pay us back gradually."

I signed a contract and took the bag of Polish money back to Poland and paid the farmer. I had been bluffing when I had told him earlier in the summer that I would return with more money, but I took it as just one more of the little miracles that are part of the work of spreading spirituality around the world.

Visit to the Baltic States and the Soviet Union

In Eastern Europe, 1990 was a big year. The year started not in January but in December of 1989 when the Berlin wall fell. In subsequent months, the seemingly formidable communist governments of Eastern Europe started to crumble. We Ananda Margis were not only spectators but participants in this process.

As early as 1967, in his book *Human Society Part II*, Baba observed that in places where communism had supplanted capitalism, "the first indications of the Vipra Age (Age of Intellectuals) are beginning to emerge." In that same book, he noted that the Hungarian revolt of 1956 was not a counter-revolution, as the Soviets asserted at the time, but a revolt of the intellectuals against a military-dominated system that had failed "because factors relating to time, place and person could not be prepared properly."

Now in early months of 1990, the factors conducive to change in Europe seemed to be more favorable. My supervisor, Dada Shambhushivananda, was invited to Lithuania where he spoke in the parliamentary session at which Lithuania proclaimed its independence from the Soviet Union. The members of this independence movement fit Baba's description exactly. They were intellectuals and their leader and the eventual first president of an independent Lithuania was Vytautas Landsbergis, a music professor.

Following Dada's first visit to Lithuania, he was invited to speak at the Second International Conference on Human Rights to be held in Vilnius, Lithuania's capital, in September 1990. Lithuania had not yet managed to become truly independent and the government in Moscow did everything they could to disrupt the coming conference. Dada and many other would-be speakers could not obtain visas to enter the Soviet Union, of which Lithuania was still a member. Also, the Soviets would not allow the conference to take place in Lithuania. The conference organizers managed to shift the venue to Leningrad.

When Dada S. found out that his visa had been denied, he asked me if I would speak at the conference in his place. "What should I speak about?" I asked. He replied that I should base my talk on the "Neo-Magna Carta," which Baba had written about in 1986. Baba said that framers of constitutions should guarantee four basic rights: "spiritual practice or Dharma, cultural legacy, education and indigenous linguistic expression." I prepared a talk based on these points and was eager to attend the conference.

I was not blacklisted in the Soviet Union, so I was able to obtain a visa. By this time, our missionaries had visited all of the Baltic States (Latvia, Lithuania, and Estonia) and Russia as well. We had an active unit in Leningrad, where the conference was going to take place. To make the most of the visit, I scheduled stops in Latvia and Lithuania, where we also had meditation units, and in Estonia, where I was to be received by an ecological activist whom I had met at the Ecotopia conference in Hungary.

In Lithuania, I was received by margis at the Vilnius train station. Lithuania looked somewhat like neighboring Poland. It had a mixture of beautiful old buildings and cobblestone streets along with the large block-like and rather unattractive high-rise tenements found all over the communist countries of Europe. We had a pleasant group meditation and dinner in a home in the country outside Vilnius.

The next stop on the trip was Riga, the capital of Latvia. Once again I was greeted by margis at the train station and taken to one of their homes where we enjoyed meditation along with a tasty vegetarian meal. While in the car with one of my hosts, I made a faux pas when I said, "This is my first time in the Soviet Union." My margi host was hurt because I mentioned the Soviet Union and not Latvia but then conceded, "Yes, we are not free yet."

Latvia reminded me of Lithuania and Poland, but the next city I visited surprised me. Tallinn, the capital of Estonia, offered a bright mixture of well-preserved old buildings dating back to the Middle Ages and modern Scandinavian architecture. Located on the Gulf of Finland, the city enjoyed a stream of tourists and regular trade with Sweden and Finland. Even though it was part of the Soviet Union, it had a prosperous look that I hadn't seen in the other Eastern European cities that I had previously visited.

I was met there by ecological activists who were trying to start a Green political and social movement. My ecological friends were more interested in the environment than in meditation but they did gather together some friends who listened as I spoke about the role that spirituality and yoga could play in the environmental movement.

Following my quick stops in the Baltic countries, I got on the train to Leningrad. Since 1977, I had been traveling by train all over Europe and I thought that I knew my way around; however, when I reached the Leningrad station I became disoriented. The layout of the tracks and entrance areas was different than what I was used to. I couldn't see any people waiting for passengers, which made me wonder whether the margis would come and pick me up. I only had a piece of paper with a single telephone number, and when I didn't see anyone waiting, I tried to call the number from a pay phone near the train tracks. The coin went into the phone but somehow it didn't work. I was wondering what to do next, but I didn't have to wonder long because a margi showed up and took me to his house. He was able to recognize me by my long beard and hair,.

The next day, I attended the first session of the Conference on Human Rights. The conference in Leningrad was a follow-up to a previous conference held in Krakow. That conference, which attracted one thousand participants, had been organized by members of the Solidarity Human Rights Commission and Polish Peace and Freedom movement. The conference in Leningrad had the blessings of the City Council and was organized by an amalgam of Soviet and Polish dissidents. I went there dressed in my full orange uniform and listened to the opening speeches. I was a bit shocked by the boldness and vehemence of the speakers who, among other things, decried the jailing of dissidents in psychiatric prisons in the Soviet Union.

Although Dada S. had been invited to the conference, our place in the program had not yet been finalized. I had to scurry around but I finally got a chance to speak. I was introduced by an American emcee who thought that I was a delegate from India. My talk was simultaneously translated into several languages, and when I mentioned that new constitutions should guarantee the right to indigenous linguistic expression, I got a round of enthusiastic applause.

On the final morning of the conference, a delegation of six US senators strode down the aisle of the main auditorium. Clad in crisp bluish suits, they were an impressive-looking bunch. Five of them sat down in the same row where I was sitting, one of them right next to me. On the stage their representative, Senator Alfonse D'Amato of New York, spoke on and on about human rights in Kosovo, a Yugoslavian province that I had not yet heard of but would visit some ten years later.

When the conference ended, my margi hosts took me around Leningrad. They showed me a number of buildings with murals of socialist realist art. In the murals, Lenin was pictured as a saint with smiling children all around him. "We were told that he was such a good man and that he never told a lie," one of the margis sheepishly said. I didn't tell him that we also were told the same thing about George Washington.

Back at the house of the margis, I began my work as a meditation teacher. At that time Leningrad was our most active center in Russia, and fifteen young men lined up to learn meditation from me. It takes anywhere from twenty minutes to an hour to teach the Ananda Marga meditation lesson to a beginner, but early on in my work I learned how to streamline the process. Whenever I have a large group of people I gather them together and explain preliminaries to them collectively. Then I call them in one by one to learn the details that are personal to them. Instead of spending fifteen hours with this particular group of people, I was able to impart the lessons in a much shorter time.

I had one last stop on my tour and that was Moscow. During my childhood, Moscow was the capital of our mortal enemy, the seat of the "Evil Empire." Now, after seeing the spirited dissidents at the Human Rights Conference, it seemed like this empire was no longer so menacing. But still I was wary. A few years earlier, one of our nuns traveled in plain clothes from Japan to Eastern Russia to teach meditation to interested youth. She was accosted and detained by the KGB, who wanted her to become their agent and spy on Japan. She was released and got back to Japan safely, but the incident was on my mind as I and an accompanying margi traveled on a night train to Moscow.

Our group in Moscow was smaller and less active than in Leningrad, but we enjoyed meditating together and shared a meal after meditation. I also got a chance to visit the city and even walked in Red Square. During the Cold War, I had read that the Soviets took the possibility of nuclear war quite seriously and were much better prepared to protect their civilian population than we were in the US. This was confirmed by my trip in the Moscow subway. Escalators took us deeper and deeper to the train platforms. The depth of the subway was much greater than I had seen in the US or in other parts of Europe, no doubt built as a way of providing shelter from an attack on the city.

Following the short stay in Moscow, I took a train back to West Germany. If Dada S. had not asked me to attend the conference in his place, I would not have had the chance to get a glimpse of the last days of the Soviet Union.

Baba's Passing

When I was in India in September, 1989, I thought that eventually I would have another chance to see Baba in India, but I was wrong. In Ananda Marga, circles there was a prevalent belief that Baba would remain in his physical body until 2005. The origin of this belief was a story told by one of the early Ananda Marga disciples. He said that he was with Baba in

1955, just after Ananda Marga had been founded, and Baba went into a very high state of consciousness and said that he would leave his body then and there. This disciple begged Baba to remain in his physical body and complete the work of establishing the social and spiritual ideals of Ananda Marga. The disciple asked Baba to stay for fifty more years, and finally, after a lot of pleading, Baba relented and said that he would stay. (This incident is described in detail in the *The Jamalpur Years*.) Everyone in Ananda Marga had heard versions of this story and most of us believed that Baba would be with us for at least fifteen more years. Even when Baba developed a heart condition and had two heart attacks, we still were not worried and went on with our work, with business as usual.

On October 21, 1990, I was in a meeting with monks and nuns in Germany when we got the news that Baba had passed away. This was astonishing to me because I really believed that Baba would be around till 2005. When I heard this news, it felt like the lights had been turned off in the room. My world turned to black. We cut short our meeting, and I went back to our headquarters in Mainz. We learned that a funeral would be held on October 26, and I wanted to go to India to attend it. I called some margis and they helped me to purchase a ticket to India.

A few days later I arrived at our headquarters in Tiljala, which was filled with margis from around the world. Baba's body was on display in a room in his residence adjacent to the headquarters building. Margis silently filed into the room and paid their last respects. The grief in the compound was extremely heavy. People were bursting into tears on and off. Baba's body lay in state from October 21 to October 26.

On October 26, a cremation ceremony took place. A large platform shaped in the form of the six-pointed star, known as *Bhaeravii Chakra* in yoga circles but exactly the same as the Star of David, was constructed in the center of the Ananda Marga compound in Tiljala. Pallbearers carried Baba's body to the center of this platform where a large pyre of wood had been constructed. Baba was placed on the pyre and it was ignited. More than five thousand margis crowded around, filling every spare inch of the walled compound. We watched the fire burn for many hours, wondering what would happen next. During this time I looked up in the sky and saw a flock of birds fly in formation over the pyre. In one coordinated motion they dipped down toward the pyre, performing a salute to Baba.

The Indian newspapers covered Baba's passing, and some reporters speculated that there would be a power struggle in the organization following the guru's departure. I scoffed at this, and in the immediate aftermath nothing happened. One of the senior monks, Acharya Shraddhananda Avadhuta, was unanimously accepted as the head of the organization.

I went back to Germany and continued with my work, grief stricken, wondering why the prophecy had seemingly failed, but as I heard more accounts of Baba's last days and reflected on Baba's life, I came to understand that there was nothing amiss. Certainly Baba would have had to leave this world one day or another, whether it was 1990 or 2005. Regardless of the date, we would have had to go on with our mission.

8
The Balkans

Now that we had a big farm in Poland, it was possible to organize programs and invite people to enjoy the beautiful environment. We received the title to the farm at the end of the summer of 1990, so it was too late to hold any programs. However, I started making plans for the following summer. While traveling to India, I had met acharyas who were working in Australia. They told me about the Ananda Mela, a festival that was held every year at their main master unit, Ananda Pali. The Ananda Mela combined workshops on Ananda Marga with general workshops on ecology, spirituality, and alternative lifestyles, along with daily sessions of chanting (kiirtan) and meditation. In addition, I had just seen the Ecotopia festival in Hungary.

I wanted to do something similar in Poland, so in the spring of 1991 I announced that we would be holding a Neohumanist Ecology Festival at our master unit, which had been given the name Ananda Putta Bhumi by Baba. One monk in India told me that when Baba gave the name to the master unit, he said, "Po-land, Putta Bhumi." *Puta* means "purified" and *bhumi* means "land." The festival was scheduled for July 14–18, 1991.

We designed some nice posters with a rustic logo that included a windmill and an apple. Some young volunteers put these posters up in several Polish cities, and we soon got letters from people who said that they were coming to the festival. Communism had just fallen and people were interested in all kinds of new activities. It was not hard to generate interest in the festival.

I organized some workshops following the formula of the Ananda Mela of Australia, combining Ananda Marga-themed classes and workshops with activities based on ecological themes. These included workshops on organic farming, bee-keeping, and natural medicine.

Getting people to come was not a problem, and providing an interesting program was also not a problem. The biggest challenge was the logistics of providing accommodation and facilities for everyone. Although the farm had a beautiful environment, the buildings were not very good. There was an old barn and an old farmhouse. I remember immediately after purchasing the property, I invited one senior margi from Warsaw to come and visit. When he saw the condition of the farmhouse, he said, "It's very tantric." That's an Ananda Marga euphemism for "very uncomfortable or rough," a physical challenge, just as the tantric path is all about challenge.

We only had one bathroom, an old kitchen, and not much indoor space in the farmhouse. The festival was supposed to be a camping festival, so we planned to dig some outhouse toilets. For the problem of the kitchen we turned to the Soviet Army, which was getting ready to leave Poland. While some shady characters in Eastern Europe were at this moment illegally purchasing rockets and other munitions from the retreating Soviet Forces, all we wanted were some tents, some folding chairs, and a portable army stove. We were able to get these items at a cheap price. We were also able to rent some big tents from a nearby fire department. So we were almost ready to hold the festival.

I say "almost ready" because we never really were able to solve the problem of how so many people would bathe, nor were we able to construct proper toilets prior to the beginning of the festival. But we went ahead anyway. More than one hundred people were inspired by our posters and advertisements and came to the farm with their backpacks and tents. The weather was also uncooperative, with rain on and off throughout the festival.

Despite all the problems, however, it proved to be a successful program. People enjoyed it, the local media loved writing newspaper articles and doing reportages for television and radio, and we felt that we had made some steps in utilizing the farm for the benefit of a wider community.

The festival was reprised the next year and every year since then, right up until today. Gradually we were able to improve the facilities. We constructed a pond, which held a lot of water, and this water was piped to a bathhouse that we constructed out of cinder blocks. The bathhouse had showers and toilets. In subsequent years, the farmhouse was renovated and the barn was converted into a large meeting hall. We also purchased the adjacent farm, which brought our total up to forty-six hectares (114 acres).

Transferred to Cairo Sector

I had returned to Europe from Japan in 1984 and continued working in various countries through 1998. However, in the first week of June

1998, I was included in a long list of transfers that were made within Ananda Marga.

It is a general principle in Ananda Marga that its monks and nuns should periodically be transferred to new places. This system has its advantages and disadvantages, both for the individual monks and nuns, and for the organization itself. The main advantage for a monk or nun is that periodic transfers create dynamism and prevent people from falling into a monotonous rut. Also, visiting, living, and working in new places are mind-expanding experiences.

At the time of the summer (May–June) meeting in Ananda Nagar, many monks and nuns who had been working in the same place for extended periods were given assignments in new locations. Since I had been in Berlin Sector (Europe) for fourteen years, my name was on the list of transfers. My new post was the public relations secretary for Cairo Sector.

Cairo Sector is the Ananda Marga designation for the countries of the Middle East, most of North Africa, and the Balkans (including Greece, Albania, and the countries of the former Yugoslavia). A posting in Cairo Sector was sometimes viewed as a "punishment posting," because at first it was very difficult to propagate Ananda Marga in the Islamic countries of the Middle East, and thus we didn't have many centers, members, or resources in that sector. Later, as the world and the Middle East in particular began to change, we did find ways to spread our ideas and practices here.

I don't really know whether monks and nuns were actually sent to Cairo Sector deliberately to face hardship due to their misdeeds or not, but it was certainly a widespread belief in some circles. That's why when I called up a margi in Norway and told him that I had been transferred to Cairo Sector, he immediately exclaimed, "Dada, what did you do?" There was also a perception that once you got to Cairo Sector there would be nothing much you could do there. When I called another margi to tell him about my transfer, he said, "But, Dada, what will you do there?" I would soon find out.

I packed my belongings in a large canvas duffel bag, got on an airplane and flew to Athens, where our sectorial headquarters was located. I was received at the airport by one of the dadas who took me by bus to an apartment that served as both our administrative headquarters and as a meditation center. I met with the sectorial secretary and we made a plan for my first few weeks in the sector. I was to make a visit to the main places where we had activities and then decide where I would settle down. The places that I visited in this first tour of the sector were Cyprus, Israel, Malta, and Croatia.

In the late 1990s, it was possible to take a ferryboat from Athens to Cyprus and then go on to Israel, so I bought a ticket and boarded the ferry to Cyprus. The ferry reached a port on the south side of the island, and from there I took a shared taxi to the capital, Nicosia, where there was an Ananda Marga center. It was late August and Cyprus was baking in the summer heat. I looked out of the taxi windows and saw a landscape that looked like it belonged on the moon. In the cooler months, that same landscape blooms with vegetation but when I traveled through it, it looked bleak.

When we finally reached the Nicosia area, the taxi took me to the Ananda Marga center. Though it was a house in a residential area, it did not have very good insulation, especially the roof, which was sheet metal, and it was really hot inside. I wondered whether it was like this in all the Cypriot houses. I met the margis, visited a piece of land outside of Nicosia that was being developed as a master unit, and generally enjoyed my first look at Cyprus.

After my brief stay in Cyprus it was time to catch the ferry to Israel. Since I grew up in a Jewish family, I was keenly interested in seeing Israel. I arrived in the port city of Haifa and after being greeted by a number of security people, I passed through immigration and took a train to Tel Aviv. There was an Ananda Marga office in Ramat Gan, an area directly adjacent to Tel Aviv proper.

Israel reminded me of Western Europe, with its apartment buildings, parks, and pedestrian shopping areas. There were margis in Tel Aviv, Jerusalem and also in Haifa, and periodically they came together for retreats. I visited Israel a few times in the next two years, attending retreats and visiting a "Green" kibbutz through a contact from *New Renaissance Magazine*. I also got a chance to visit Jerusalem and went to the holy sites of the city.

In September of 1998, I continued my initial tour of the sector with the Mediterranean island nation of Malta. There were a lot of margis in Malta and they were high spirited. During the kiirtan, I couldn't hear my guitar because the singing and drumming was so loud.

I concluded the tour with a visit to Croatia. Croatia had been part of Yugoslavia but broke away in a bloody war in 1992. It is a Catholic country, as is Malta, and Ananda Marga seems to do well in Catholic countries. Once again I found a lot of margis here, just as I had in Malta and a decade before in Poland.

After the tour I went back to our office in Athens, and after some consultation with the sectorial secretary, I decided to make my initial base in Cyprus. I settled in our house there, which during the cooler weather was actually not so bad, and remained till the early part of 1999. We held yoga classes at our center and even had a small seminar during the sunny days of March.

The Dadas of Cairo Sector

Nine Years in Albania

I was getting ready to settle for a while in Cyprus when international events intruded. In April 1999, the long-festering ethnic problems in the Serbian province of Kosovo exploded. This province was inhabited by a majority population of ethnic Albanians practicing Islam, but it was also an area that was historically important for the Serbs, who were Orthodox Christians. When hostilities between the two ethnic groups erupted, the Serbs forced six hundred thousand ethnic Albanians to flee the province, and they sought refuge in neighboring Albania. This created a humanitarian problem for Albania, a small and impoverished country. As the armies of NATO started bombing Yugoslavia, hoping to bring about a military solution to the problem, hundreds of non-governmental relief organizations poured into Albania trying to provide relief assistance to the refugees.

From our Athens headquarters, we organized a branch of our Ananda Marga Universal Relief Team and sent it to Tirana to help with the relief effort. In a very short time our team was able to set up two offices and a warehouse, and soon we were feeding thousands of refugees each day. We already had monks, nuns, and volunteers working there when I was asked to join the team.

I traveled from Athens to Tirana, the capital of Albania, by bus, a long and uncomfortable journey. If my bus ride in Nepal in 1981 was the bus ride from hell, then this was the sequel. The streets of Tirana were clogged with traffic, including the SUVs and other vehicles of the various relief agencies. I participated in the relief activities of our team for a few weeks and enjoyed it. We even played basketball with some of the refugees and found them to be congenial people. However, as we got to know them better, we realized that the region was not going to experience real peace for a long time to come. One of them told me what he wanted to do when he returned to Kosovo: "We've got to kill the Gypsies and the Serbs," he said. According to him, the Roma people (Gypsies) in Kosovo had allied themselves with the Serbs in the drive to oust the ethnic Albanians from the province, and that was how he expressed his bitterness.

In the middle of May, everything changed abruptly. The NATO bombing campaign succeeded in driving the Serbian army out of Kosovo, and the thousands of refugees in Albania returned to their homes almost as fast as they had fled. That was good news for Albania, but it was a bit disorienting for our relief workers. We had two offices, a warehouse filled with relief materials, and various staff members but no clear idea of what we were going to do next. Eventually we sent some monks and nuns back to Athens and other parts of our sector, but I stayed on in Tirana to manage our office.

There was one main margi in Tirana and one newcomer who quickly became a staunch practitioner of meditation and an active member of our organization. They helped me to organize some interesting post-refugee-crisis activities in Albania, and these activities kept me busy for the next nine years.

One of the new margis was a former finance minister who had a good grasp of the problems the country was facing. He pointed me to Bathore, a district just outside the capital. According to him, thousands of residents of Albania's northern provinces had fled to the Tirana area in 1992, following the collapse of state-run industries in the upheaval that ended forty-five years of communist rule. Some of these internal refugees settled in a vast agricultural tract that became the informal village of Bathore. There were few government services in the area and some of the residents lived in converted cattle sheds. "Bathore is a ticking time-bomb," he said, emphasizing that the area was in need of social service.

I wasn't really sure what I could do to help the people of this community, but I was willing to look into the problem. Fortunately, I was not alone. Another monk was working with me and we had good contacts in the other non-governmental relief organizations. In fact, I met an old friend in Albania, Wam Kat, the Dutch national whom I had met during the ecology festival in Hungary, the same man who helped me with a loan for the master unit in Poland in 1990! He was in Albania with his organization "Balkan Sunflowers," and I became friends and partners with his team.

Together with the Balkan Sunflowers, we sent an exploratory team to Bathore, which was only a short bus ride from Tirana. Members of the Balkan Sunflowers decided to start an after-school program for children. At the time, I didn't see how I could contribute to that effort, but events were to prove me wrong.

More promising was the interest that a few of the Balkan Sunflowers showed in starting a microcredit program for Bathore. "Microcredit" is the term given to small loans for people who want to start or expand business enterprises that will help them to become economically self-sufficient. They were made famous by Mohamad Yunus, a Bangladeshi professor who discovered that by giving loans as small as twenty-seven dollars he could help struggling villagers buy hens and start an egg-production business. Yunus went on to found the Grameen Bank, which specialized in this kind of micro-business lending.

We set up a joint team to plan a program for Bathore, targeting the part of the district that seemed to be in most need of our help. It was the area where some families were still living in converted cattle sheds. Others lived in hastily constructed homes that didn't have proper plumbing, sewage and other utilities. We struck up a friendship with Fatmir, an elected elder in that area, and this friendship proved to be the key to getting our microcredit program off the ground.

A second important factor that made it possible to turn our plans into realities was a donation that was given to one of the members of the Balkan Sunflowers team. She lived in California and was a member of a Quaker community there. Her community raised ten thousand dollars for the microcredit program. Due to internal matters within the Balkan Sunflowers, the donation was given to our Ananda Marga Universal Relief Team to administer.

We now had a fund and a trusted member of the community to help us find qualified people who could make use of loans. All we needed was some help with the mechanism of making the loans and monitoring the repayment. Our margi, the former finance minister, was now a consultant to one of the important banks in Tirana, and we were able to work out an arrangement where the fund would be deposited in that bank, and our loan recipients would make their payments directly to the bank.

Once we were ready to begin, Fatmir spread the word in the community, and we held a meeting with the people who wanted to get loans. A number of people wanted to set up small shops selling groceries and supplies, since there were few such shops in the area. Another person wanted to buy a van to start a passenger-transport service. Someone wanted some extra money to inject into a concrete-block manufacturing facility, and a group of women wanted money to buy looms so that they could weave traditional Albanian carpets. We were ready to provide small loans to these people, and a member of the bank helped us to evaluate the loan applicants and set the limit for the amounts that could be borrowed based on their family income and expenses and the anticipated income that the business would generate.

The program was successful beyond our expectations. We cycled the ten thousand dollars through the system more than four times, giving initial loans and then giving further rounds of loans to new participants as well as to the original recipients who had repaid their loans. Of the total forty thousand dollars and some two hundred loans, everything was repaid except for seventy dollars which was owed by a man who was unsuccessful in establishing a transport business with his van.

One of the microcredit recipients weaving traditional Albanian carpets

Once the microcredit project took off, I began looking for other ways to be of service in Bathore. I heard that several people in the community wanted to learn English so I offered to teach them. When I was in Japan and Taiwan I had taught English from time to time in order to raise money. In Albania, I did it purely as a service activity. I had a some grateful students who developed their English skills quite a bit in the next few years.

The Albanian Sunrise School

A big part of the Ananda Marga mission is to open ideal schools. In India, Ananda Marga has started and continues to operate hundreds of schools ranging from nursery to college level. The educational method in these schools, known as Neohumanist Education (see www.gurukul.edu for more information), combines progressive education methods with meditation.

Starting schools outside of India proved to be more difficult, especially in developed countries, which have more stringent requirements for new schools. In spite of this, there are now Ananda Marga schools throughout the world. In Cairo Sector, we were not very successful in setting up schools. However, in 1999 during a meeting with my fellow monks in Athens, I said that if I had a bit of financial backing I could open a school.

My colleagues agreed to help out with some modest financial support and I went back to Albania to see how I could carry out my plan. I went to Bathore and discussed the school with the Fatmir, the village elder. He took me around the area and we identified buildings that might be suitable. We didn't have a big budget to work with, but eventually we found an unused room adjacent to the living area of a local family. It wasn't ideal but we had to begin somewhere.

Next I needed a teacher. Fatmir again came to the rescue and introduced me to a woman who had a teaching credential and was looking for a job. I interviewed her and decided that she would be suitable for the undertaking.

All that was needed now were some students. As it turned out, the local government school was overcrowded—it could only provide kindergarten education for a few of the thousands of residents of Bathore. I met with some of the parents and we selected twenty children for our first class. The parents would pay a few dollars a month to help defray the costs of paying the teacher and renting the room; however, the fees collected from the parents did not cover all of our expenses, which was why the support from the other monks was so important.

On October 2, 2000, our school, which we called the Albanian Sunrise School, opened its doors to the first group of children, ages four through six. I was happy with what we had accomplished, but after a few days I met the village elder and he said that we had "a problem." I was expecting bad news, but it turned out that the problem was that there were more parents who wanted to enroll their children in our kindergarten. The solution was to build a new room, an extension to the building that we were renting as our first classroom. The expenses were manageable and we began the construction work. Now I needed to find another teacher. The wife of one of my English students was already teaching in a local kindergarten and I asked her if she would like to join our project. She agreed to join us, and very soon we had two classes with a total of forty children who were now off the streets and in a classroom.

Our goal was to make this school special by using the Ananda Marga methods of Neohumanist Education. During that period, I employed an Albanian assistant who began translating a thick book entitled *The Circle of Love*. *The Circle of Love* is a detailed teacher's manual organized in a way that reflects the Ananda Marga worldview. There are stories, exercises, and everything else a teacher needs to give lessons throughout the year. Once the translation was ready, our teachers began to use the Albanian edition of *Circle of Love* to shape their lessons. I also made it a point to bring my guitar and sing songs with the children on a regular basis. Through the songs, the children were able to begin learning English, and we finished our singing sessions with silent meditation. My guitar playing, singing, and mantra chanting proved to be a very valuable part of the school routine.

After our first year, we were able to see good results from our efforts. The pupils who completed our course went on to first grade in the local public school, and we learned that they were performing very well. In fact, in subsequent years, some of the public school teachers came to our school to "recruit" children to enroll in their classes.

One of my weekly music sessions at the kindergarten.

Internet Marketing, Music and Songwriting

In 2002 my life took another turn in a seemingly surprising direction. I began writing songs, recording them with other musicians, and performing them in public. I say seemingly surprising, because we yogis know that everything we do is a result of our samskaras, the unfulfilled momentum from the past. Nothing happens without a prior cause or background. This past momentum did not force me to become a performer but when the circumstances lined up in the right way, I chose my path in a manner that satisfied an inner longing.

How did this come about? Although our school program was successful in educating poor kids, it was not financially viable. The parents couldn't pay the fees that would have been needed to cover the salaries of the teachers and the rent on the school building. In the beginning, I got financial aid from some of the monks who were working with me in Cairo Sector. But this help was only temporary. Since Albania is a poor country and because I did not have enough contacts there to maintain a steady stream of donations, I began looking for another way to bridge the gap between the school's income and its expenses.

My best solution was to set up a website where I could promote myself as an expert in Internet marketing. By working on the website of *New*

Renaissance Magazine, www.ru.org, I had gained valuable experience in optimizing web pages so they would appear prominently when someone made a query in search engines. I put this expertise to use in this new business. Working from a small office in Albania, I was able to get clients (mostly from the USA), and this stream of income allowed me to both support myself and keep the school running. The idea of setting up a search-engine-optimization enterprise turned out to be a great idea.

During the years I was in Albania, I spent a lot of time on the computer and on the Internet, working on this marketing business. However, Albania was a country with severe energy problems. Their electricity was supplied by hydroelectric installations in the north of the country, but they could not meet the demand of a growing economy. On top of this, droughts limited the amount of electricity that these hydroelectric stations could provide. The energy shortfalls meant that electricity did not run continuously. During the winter of 2001 and 2002, the power cuts were particularly severe, and for most of the day I could not work at my computer. (Winter was the time of peak power demands because most of the apartments in Albania did not have central heating systems, and everyone used electric space heaters.) It was then that I came up with the idea of helping support the kindergarten by recording a CD of spiritual songs and selling it within the Ananda Marga community. But as many independent musicians can tell you, recording music to use as a fund raiser is not so easy. In fact, from the standpoint of making money, it is a bad idea.

At first I thought about recording songs written by other people. I used to sing and play a few pop songs, ones that fit my own feelings and outlook on the world. Songs like "My Sweet Lord" by George Harrison and the hippie anthem "Get Together," a song the Youngbloods made famous in 1969. I started practicing songs like this, but when the winter power cuts came and I had time on my hands with no running computer, I did something else. I took out a pen and paper and began to write my own songs. I had always admired people who could write songs, though I had never done it myself. For example, when I was in Washington, D.C. and managing the *Sadvipra* newspaper, I met a margi musician named Shivam from Alabama. A social service trainee at the Washington center, Shivam was an accomplished country and western musician who started to write spiritual songs. He put Ananda Marga themes to melodious, country-style tunes, including one song that I still sing from time to time: "Let's Not Wait Till Tomorrow."

I used to think that if I could write even one song like Shivam's song, then I would be a happy man. So I started writing songs. I wanted them to be spiritual songs but with lyrics that would not limit them to Ananda Marga listeners—in other words, cross-over *bhajans*. These would be songs that some listeners would recognize as inspiring spiritual songs, and others would understand on whatever level they could.

For example, I wrote the song "I Can Never Be Apart From You" with the following lines:

> *You're the silence in the center of a storm*
> *You're the fire that keeps my heart warm*
> *You're watching everything that I do*
> *I can never be apart from you.*

I didn't specify who the "you" is, so the song can be understood in various ways.

I also wrote about social issues. In 1979 when I walked with Baba along the Rhône River in France, I was struck by Baba's remark that there are people in the world who are suffering so much that they are not able to even voice their problems, and that we should speak for them. Based on this remark, I wrote the song "As the World Spins Around," which begins with these lines:

> *There're some people in this world without any voice*
> *There're some people in this world without any choice*
> *And they toil day and night, stuck in their plight*
> *As the world spins around,*
> *As the world spins around.*

Some of the songs included common pieces of yoga wisdom in an easy-to-understand format. In India's epic poem *The Ramayana,* there is an interesting passage in which the hero Rama slays his adversary Ravana. Rama was portrayed as an incarnation of God and Ravana was supposed to be an extremely evil person. Yet, when Ravana was wounded and was about to die, Rama, respecting his status as a senior person, requested that he give some advice from his life that would be valuable to future generations. Ravana replied that when he was a young man, he had some good ideas. He wanted to build a stairway to heaven so that people could easily reach the celestial realm. Ravana lamented that he delayed doing this good work, and now that he was dying it would never be done. He then said that when he got older he had a bad idea, namely the idea to kidnap

Rama's wife, Sita. This he put into practice immediately without thinking of the consequences, which resulted in the war described in *The Ramayana* that ultimately led to Ravana's death. Based on these events, Ravana gave his advice to Rama and to future generations: Whenever you have good things to do, do them immediately; and whenever you get an idea to do something that is not good (that will cause harm to you or to others) then delay; and when the delay period expires, delay again.

In my song "The Wise Ones Say," I tried to capture Ravana's advice in this chorus:

> *If you've got something good, do it today*
> *Gonna do something bad, make a delay.*
> *This is what the wise ones say*
> *This is what the wise ones say.*

I wrote the lyrics first and then sat down with my guitar to bring them to life as songs. While writing I used a brainstorming technique. I suspended my critical judgment and didn't try to analyze whether the lyrics were "good" or "bad." I just tried to compose a poem with an even meter so that I could put it to music.

The most popular in this first series of songs turned out to be a song about vegetarianism. In 2002 I was visiting the Ananda Marga children's home in Romania, which had been opened in the aftermath of the revolution that deposed the communist dictator Nicolae Ceaușescu in 1990. The world soon learned that this dictator tried to build up the Romanian population and army through various social policies that resulted in a large number of orphans who were kept in appalling conditions at large government-run orphanages. Several organizations, including Ananda Marga, tried to alleviate this situation by setting up smaller, more humane children's homes. Ananda Marga set up a group home near Bucharest and it was a success.

One of the features of this home was that the children were served a vegetarian diet. This was not a problem for anyone, but in the late 1990s the mood in Romania began to change and there was increasing opposition to groups like Ananda Marga that did not fit in the mainstream of the Christian religion. Because of this new anti-sect climate, the policies of the children's home came under attack. The government ordered that Ananda Marga serve meat in the children's home. I was there at the time when Ananda Marga was not only battling against this new dietary demand of the government but also successfully challenged a government website that slandered Ananda Marga. I thought that we needed a vegetarian fight song and quickly wrote these lyrics:

> *Animals are my friends and I treat them nice*
> *I spare their lives eating veggies and rice.*
> *That's why I don't eat meat, I don't eat flesh*
> *I'm trying to do my very best.*

Other verses of the song went on to give the health and ecological reasons why we are vegetarians.

The music I composed was simple, since my music background was limited. I learned guitar back in 1966 so that I could play popular folk and rock tunes, and I later started playing simple spiritual songs and chants at Ananda Marga functions. The songs I began to write were the product of my upbringing, which consisted mostly of listening to American pop music of the 1950s and 1960s. This music was heavily influenced by the folk, country, and blues music that preceded rock n roll, and my songs reflected this.

After completing a number of songs, I made a demonstration tape on an old cassette deck. I sent one copy of the cassette to my colleague Dada Gunamuktananda, who was in charge of Ananda Marga's work in Malta. He organized a concert for me in Malta in December 2002 as a benefit concert for the Albanian Sunrise School. I was backed up by a complete electric rock band and it was an exciting event. After the concert, Dada G came up to me and said, "Go for it." So I continued with my quest, trying to do something more with the songs.

The next step was to find someone who could help me to record the songs so that we could produce a CD. After making inquiries in Albania, I found a young musician who had recording software on his computer. He worked in a TV studio and was able to borrow very good microphones. He started recording my vocals and guitar accompaniment in the bedroom of his home in Tirana, after which he added percussion. One of his friends was an accomplished guitarist and he added guitar solos and bass to the songs.

Previously this kind of recording could only be done in a studio, but by 2002 digital-recording software was available to everyone. Anyone with a computer and a microphone could start recording multi-tracked songs and editing them directly at home. After about six months of once-a-week recording sessions, we had thirteen songs ready to be put on CD. I gave the album the title *Brighter than the Sun*, which was the title of the first song. We made two hundred copies and in the summer of 2003 I went to Germany and the US to take part in large Ananda Marga gatherings. I introduced my songs there and sold my CDs. By the time the summer tour was over, I had sold all two hundred copies.

I started the music project thinking about selling a few copies at Ananda Marga functions, but then I thought that maybe it could be a way to bring social and spiritual ideas to a wider public. My official monastic name, Acharya Vedaprajinananda Avadhuta, presented a challenge. Not many people could pronounce it or understand it. Even I misspell it from time to time. So for the sake of making my music more accessible, I used a shortened version, Dada Veda, on the CD and on the Internet, opening up a website at www.dadaveda.com.

Divine Moon Festival and musical revival

After the excitement of making the first CD and performing at the retreats in Germany and the US, my musical "career" entered a quiet stage. I got one or two emails from people who had bought the CD and really liked it, but beyond that there was only silence. I was discouraged. I thought that perhaps I should give it up and forget about the music. Then I heard that some margis in Portland, England were organizing a spiritual music festival, the Divine Moon Festival. I wanted to take part, though I was not sure if they would want me to perform. At this point I got into a conversation with Jishnu, a young man whom I have known since his birth in France in 1978. He encouraged me to attend, so I contacted the organizer and he put me on the bill.

Just before the Divine Moon Festival, I attended the Ananda Marga retreat in Germany. There I met Brian, a margi from England who is an accomplished fiddle player. He liked my music and we practiced together and performed at the retreat. We teamed up again at the Divine Moon Festival where we were also joined by a bass player, Rasaviharii. With the addition of Brian's fiddle, the music really fit the mold of country and western music—or rather, as one of the listeners at Divine Moon said, "county and eastern music." We played a few sets at the festival and our last set was a lively one with an encouraging audience clapping and singing along. This set was videotaped and several of the songs are still available on YouTube.com

After the good reception at the Divine Moon Festival, I became energized again and sought ways to continue writing, recording and performing my songs.

At the Divine Moon Festival, Portland, England, 2006

Syria, Jordan, Lebanon and Egypt

Although I had been in Cairo Sector for a number of years, I had not yet seen several important Middle Eastern Countries and was glad when the opportunities arose to visit these places.

One surprising bubbling center of interest in yoga and meditation was Syria. Although the country was tightly ruled by a dynastic family dictatorship and is a predominantly Islamic country, some of our teachers connected with a community that was thirsty for our style of spirituality. The Druze people are a religious group living in Syria, Lebanon, Jordan, and Israel. They emerged in the eleventh century as a faith distinct from their Islamic neighbors. They have a mystical bent of mind and share with Ananda Marga a belief that God is both transcendent and immanent in the universe around us.

When our monks first visited Syria they taught meditation to some members of this community, and soon more and more people joined them. By the time I visited Syria in 2005 and 2006, there were active Ananda Marga centers in predominantly Druze areas in the south of Syria and in the Damascus suburb of Jaramana. When I joined Ananda Marga in

1970, most of the meditators in the US were in their twenties. We did not have many older or younger members. However, in Syria I found whole families from grandparents to toddlers all practicing Ananda Marga yoga. It was amazing and truly inspiring.

At this time one of our monks was traveling all around the country dressed in his bright orange robes. This was done with the full knowledge of a regime that tracked the movement of everyone very strictly. For example, when I took a bus ride from Damascus to the city of Sweida, everyone, foreigners and nationals, had to show their passports or identification documents.

The government definitely knew we were there but they let us operate freely. In 2005 we held a seminar in a prominent auditorium in the center of Damascus with several monks and nuns in full uniform; it was filmed and shown on the main state-run television station. Some of the margis told us that the government let us work because their biggest fear was not yoga and meditation from India, but Islamic fundamentalism and extremism from their own region. Unfortunately, this period of grace did not last long. After a few years our monks and nuns could not get their visas renewed and the entire country descended into civil war.

Seminar in Damascus, 2005

But while it lasted it was beautiful. Hospitality in Syrian homes was amazing and we were treated to the wonderful cuisine that the country is known for. Lots of fresh salad, olives, cheeses, breads and sweets more than satisfied us. We held retreats and also enjoyed excursions to scenic sites, such as a Roman amphitheater in the southern city of Bosra, as well as the famous Umayyad Mosque of Damascus.

Jordan and Egypt

We did not have many activities in Syria's neighbor Jordan except for occasional seminars and yoga classes in Amman, but we held a retreat there in 2007. The retreat took place in a campsite near Wadi Rum, one of the chief tourist destinations in Jordan. Wadi Rum, the Valley of the Moon, is a valley in South Jordan sixty miles east of the port city of Aqaba. In ancient times it was inhabited by the Nabateans, a trading people who left behind a magnificent city built right into a steep mountainside. In modern times Wadi Rum was the home of T.E. Lawrence's military campaign against the Ottoman Turks in World War I, which was immortalized in the film *Lawrence of Arabia*. Taking advantage of time before and after the retreat, we visited some of the tourist attractions along with margis of Syria, Malta, Cyprus, Jordan, and Lebanon. We rode camels in the desert, slept at a Bedouin camp, saw the ruins of fortresses used by T.E. Lawrence, marveled at the architecture of the Nabatean city of Petra, floated in the Dead Sea, and stood at Mount Nebo on the very spot where Moses is said to have viewed the Holy Land before passing away. The natural beauty of the Jordanian deserts and mountains was astounding, and meditating in the desert was a unique experience.

The retreat itself was beautiful. The coming together of people from so many different Middle Eastern countries gave me the hope that one day peace will come to this troubled part of the world.

In the Jordanian desert near Wadi Rum

Dada Gunaragananda (left), the author, and Dada Krsnasevananda standing in front of T.E. Lawrence's fortress in Wadi Rum, Jordan

Although our sector was given the name Cairo Sector by Baba, we did not have a big presence in Egypt's capital. We owned a small apartment in a locality we called "Chicken Street" because on the ground floor of our building there was a large shop that kept and slaughtered poultry. One of our monks stationed in Cairo gave yoga classes in various studios around the city but we did not have a large local following of meditators.

At the end of 2005, we held our periodic meeting of monks and nuns in Cairo. It was my first visit to the African continent and I came with eyes wide open. In addition to holding our meetings, we also visited the Great Pyramids of Giza, the Sphinx, which is right next to the Pyramids, and the Egyptian museum in downtown Cairo. Our host monk also took us to some of his yoga classes where we gave short talks and performed some songs.

Our dada in Egypt also organized a concert for me in an open-air theater next to the Nile River. Dada P. did his best to publicize the concert but only a handful of friends showed up for the event. I started performing but due to the lighting I could not really see who was in the audience. While I was singing some people who worked at the theater sat down and listened. When I finished, they came up to me and said, "Can you sing some Cat Stevens songs?"—not surprising since Cat Stevens converted to Islam and I imagine he must have a good following in this part of the world.

One or two visits to a country do not make me or anyone else an expert but while I was in Egypt two images struck my mind. At the time of prayer, the mosques in downtown Cairo filled to overflowing. People with prayer mats crowded the streets around the mosques and everything around them stopped. A contrasting view of Egypt came at the huge Carrefour market just outside the city, where Dada P. brought us for some shopping. In France they call such markets *hypermarchés* or hypermarkets and this place lived up to that name. The store stretched over thousands of square feet and was stocked with all the goods you would find in Europe or North America. Egyptians there were just as avid about their shopping as their compatriots on the prayer mats in downtown Cairo were about their religion. I could see that the struggle in Egypt today is in large part a conflict about reconciling old beliefs with the forces of modernity.

9

Back to Brooklyn

During my last years in Cairo Sector, composing and performing music became one of my biggest interests, but it was difficult to play my kind of music, with its English lyrics, in Albania where I spent most of my time. That's why I jumped at a chance, in the summer of 2007, to ride on the Kundalini Express for a tour of music festivals in the US. The Kundalini Express was an old yellow school bus that some members of Ananda Marga bought. They took out the rear seats and converted the back into a sleeping area. Colorfully decorated on the outside, it resembled the hippie buses of the late 1960s and early 1970s. No wonder it drew some interesting looks from tourists when we took it through midtown Manhattan at the start of our journey.

The tour was led by youths in their twenties. Back in 1970, young people were the only kind of margis you could find, but forty years later there were older folks like myself as well as this up-and-coming new generation who wanted to spread spirituality throughout the country.

They arranged a visit to festivals such as Floyd Fest in Virginia and the Transformus Festival in North Carolina. There were also open-air concerts in Asheville, North Carolina, and Knoxville, Tennessee, as well as events in New England. I performed with young musicians who sang background vocals on my songs and accompanied me on different instruments.

My experience from the sixties came in handy on the tour. When we reached the gates of the Transformus Festival, people on the bus were shocked. Some of the greeters at this avant-garde festival were completely naked! I remained calm and said that we should enter anyway and see what happens. It turned out to be a good event, and I was able to teach meditation to a few young men.

After the summer festival tour ended, I went back to Albania but that was not the end of my involvement with my native land. For the past several years, I had been asked by some people in Ananda Marga if I could help out with the propagation of the movement in the US. I wasn't interested at first, but as my involvement in spreading spirituality through music grew, the idea became more attractive. Finally in September of 2008, after ten years in Cairo sector, mostly in Albania, I packed my bags and returned to the USA, making my base in the Ananda Marga headquarters in Queens, not far from my birthplace in Brooklyn. After more than thirty years abroad, I was back in the US, not just for a quick visit but for an extended period.

Our office in Queens was in a multifamily house that Ananda Marga had purchased in 1980s and later renovated. When I was growing up in Brooklyn in the 1950s, Queens was thought of as a suburban residential area with the lawns, trees and gardens that urban Brooklyn lacked. Many middle-class families flocked to Queens and later Long Island to buy homes. The Queens of 2008 was not like this 1950s dream vision. It was a crowded, multiethnic urban community. Our office was located in a Spanish-speaking area.

After getting settled in my new accommodations, I began to travel. I went to the southeastern part of the US, visiting Atlanta and a few places in North Carolina. I gave a lecture at the state university in New Paltz, New York, and even made a trip to Nicaragua and Costa Rica, where Ananda Marga has considerable activities. When I was not traveling, I tried to do something productive in the New York City area.

Concert in Knoxville during the Kundalini Express Tour of 2007

Bar Prachar

One day at the beginning of my career as a monk in Europe, my supervisor shocked me when he asked, "Have you ever gone into the bars where the young people drink and dance and try to meet people interested in meditation?" What a crazy question, I thought, but I quietly replied no. Thirty years later, I did indeed start entering bars, not to drink but to share my music and spirituality. I never thought it would happen but it did. I wanted to perform music as much as I could, and one way to do that was by singing at open mics. Open mics are evenings at cafes, bars and clubs where anyone can sign up on a list and perform for about ten to fifteen minutes. I checked the Internet and found many such opportunities in the New York area.

When I checked the open-mic listings, I noticed almost all of these sessions took place at bars. I wanted to avoid the bars, thinking the atmosphere would not be right for me, that it would be odd for an orange-robed yogi to mingle there. So I carefully sifted through the listings and found one open mic held in a coffeehouse in Brooklyn. I went to the coffeehouse and performed. It went well enough for me to consider going to more open mics. But there were no more coffeehouse open mics to choose from, so I had to try some of the bars.

The first bar that I visited was the Sidewalk Café in New York's East Village. This bar is a well-known music spot; its Monday-night open mic is packed with singer-songwriters and other entertainers, and their open mic session runs into the wee hours of the night, well past the bedtime of a yogi.

At the Sidewalk Café, they use a lottery system to determine who will perform at what time. The would-be performers line up in front of a table where an employee takes down their name and holds up two fists, asking them to choose one. Then he opens his fist, looks at something and gives them a number. When my turn at the table came, he was taken aback to see a turbaned, orange-robed yogi. He opened the fist that I had chosen and told me my number was twenty-five.

I sat down but soon realized that I wouldn't be on for another six hours or so and the first performer was going to begin at 8:00 PM. I knew I didn't want to wait till 2:00 AM but I just sat there wondering what to do. After some time, the person in charge of the selection process came to me and said, "Well, since you're new here we can give you a break." He gave me a lower number and I was able to perform at around 10:00 PM. I was only given time to perform one song so I did "As the World Spins Around." It got a good reception and the next week when I went back there I got a very low number when I chose one of the clenched fists. (I believe they gave the numbers out arbitrarily according to their whims and personal likes and dislikes, but I can't prove it.)

After having played at the famous Sidewalk Café, I had enough confidence to walk into any bar and perform. On a cold night two days before Christmas 2008, I went to an open mic in a basement theater at St. Mark's Place in the East Village. Forty years earlier I had often walked up and down St. Mark's Place, which was then the main hangout for the hippies of New York City.

The counterculture aura of 1968's St. Mark's Place was kept alive in this theater. The basement theater was dimly lit and the first thing I did was to enter my name in a lottery. This was a real lottery—the names were chosen from a box. I got a high number but decided to stay. I put my guitar in a storage area in the back and sat down to watch the show until my number was called.

It was a wild show indeed. One performer had devil's horns attached to his head and another performer "psychoanalyzed" him. A dancer went onstage adorned only in Christmas tree lights. There was a lot of beer consumed by the audience and the performers, and the smell of the beer on the floor reminded me of the basement of my fraternity house in college. It was definitely not a yogic setting and I wanted to leave as soon as I could.

At around 11:00 PM there was an intermission. I realized that it was a good opportunity to make my escape. I tiptoed to the storage area and got my guitar. As I was walking out, the woman who was hosting the event stopped me and said, "Oh, we really wanted to hear you perform." She said that I could perform right after the break, which was enough to convince me to stay.

Shortly after 11:00 PM, I took the stage and the first thing I did was to explain myself. "I am dressed this way because I am a yoga teacher." Everyone started clapping, which put me at ease. I then performed a song and got a good response from the audience. When the song was over I asked the host how much time I had left. This particular open mic had a strict six-minute allowance for each performer. They told me that I had two minutes and forty six seconds left. I realized that this was not enough time for a song so I told a short spiritual tale.

"I had a college roommate who became one of the most respected Zen Buddhist teachers in America," I began. (This was true—one of my roommates during my semester in London became a teacher who has written many books and won public recognition.) "Compared to him, I am nobody." I then launched into the tale of an incident at a Jewish synagogue somewhere in Europe.

"One day the rabbi of that synagogue wanted to impress his congregation," I began. "He threw himself on the floor before the altar and started wailing. 'Lord, I am nobody, Lord, I am nobody.' The cantor saw this and was impressed. He also threw himself to the ground and began saying, 'Lord, I'm nobody, Lord, I am nobody.' The two of them continued to repeat 'Lord, I am nobody' over and over again, until the janitor in the hallway got curious and looked inside the worship room. He was impressed by what he saw and heard, so he also flung himself to the floor beside the two clergymen and joined in, wailing, 'Lord, I'm nobody. At this point the cantor became annoyed and said to the rabbi, 'And look who thinks he is nobody!'"

The audience started laughing and clapping. All in all, it was a successful performance in a place that at first glance didn't appear to be a good setting for my music and spirituality.

I bid farewell to everyone as the applause continued and made my way in the frigid December night to the subway station a few blocks away. While I was waiting for my train back to Queens, I struck up a conversation with a man who inquired about my guitar, which was in an odd-sized case. He was wondering what kind of instrument it was. It turned out that the man was in a spiritual music ensemble in New York. We became friends and kept in touch for a long time afterward.

Mic Club and Love is the Best

Sometime in January 2009, I went to an open mic evening that was a bit more congenial than the one at the basement theater on St. Mark's Street. Lucky Jacks is a boisterous bar on New York's Lower East Side. The street-level bar caters to young people in their twenties and thirties. Two television sets show the games of New York sports teams and there is a lot of conversation and clanking of beer bottles. It wouldn't seem like the kind of place for a yogi-musician; however, every Thursday the basement section of Lucky Jacks hosted Mic Club. Mic Club is the brainchild of Sacha Chavez and his partner, Frances Ann. Unlike many open mic hosts, Sacha Chavez is flamboyant and very welcoming. His concept of music and art is remarkably similar to the approach put forward in Ananda Marga's

Renaissance Artists and Writers Association (RAWA), which states that art should be an instrument for service and spiritual elevation.

When I showed up at Lucky Jacks, Sacha gave me a warm introduction and I played two songs. I kept coming back each Thursday and started to make friends with a number of musicians and comedians. One of the comedians said to me in typical New York City style, "After listening to you, I hate less." Another of the stand-up comics got up on the stage after one of my performances and said, "Actually, I'm a plainclothes disciple of the previous performer."

During this period when I was going to various venues to perform, I was also looking for a way to make another recording. I was not satisfied with the first CD that we made in Albania and still had a number of songs that had never been recorded. One day I was putting new strings on my guitar when one of the bridge pins became jammed. I couldn't do anything with it, so I took the guitar to a big music shop in Queens. They fixed the pin and the guitar was fine. On the way out, I noticed a business card on the bulletin board advertising recording services, so I called the number, hoping to find someone to help me produce another CD.

The person who picked up the phone was a Danish musician who agreed to work with me at a very reasonable rate. His name was Ryan Sambleben, or Ryan Sam as he is known in performance circles. Ryan was a skilled singer, keyboardist, guitarist and bass player who was making his living giving piano and voice lessons. He had a small studio in a garage at the back of his house in Queens, about two miles from our Ananda Marga office, and he was eager to produce my songs.

When I went to see him, I took out my guitar and played a song. He made a rough recording of the song and told me to come back in one week. When I came back he had made a full backing track complete with guitar, piano, bass, and percussion. I listened to the instrumental track with headphones and then added my vocal parts. We did this for each of the songs on the CD. Ryan was a vocal coach, and since he had already recorded the complete instrumental arrangements of the songs, I was able to concentrate on the vocal parts, and I was satisfied with how they came out.

The title song of the CD was "Love is the Best." I recorded the song in 2009 but I wrote it in 2003, when I was still in Albania running the Sunrise School. In June of that year, a young Bolivian-American, Gustavo Monje, came to Albania to work as an intern in the school. I introduced him to the teachers and each day he would help out in the school. One day Gustavo returned to our office in Tirana and said, "I created a new song for the kids at the school." The song was a simple refrain accompanied by hand gestures, making it perfect for sing-alongs with the kids. It went like this: "I love you," with both hands and arms extended out in front; "I love me," with hands folded in, pointing to your chest; " I love you" repeated again; "I love me" repeated; and then the closing line, "love is the best," with both hands raised high over the head.

The kids loved the song and the gestures. Gustavo had to leave after a short time at the school, but I kept singing it with the kids for the next five years. One day I thought, "This is a good song. Maybe I should add some lyrics and record it." I added three verses and performed it at some events in Sweden. It turned out to be a crowd-pleaser. Everyone enjoyed singing along and making the hand and arm movements.

"Love is the Best" was recorded in Ryan Sam's studio and the title track was complemented by ten other songs. I like all of the songs I put on a CD but inevitably there are a few that stand out. They are the ones most requested and the ones I like to perform more often. A few of the songs I recorded with Ryan became "hits" in this sense of the word.

Two of them share the same theme but were written a few years apart. In 2002 I was in Malta, getting ready to go to an appointment. I had to wait for another person to get ready before leaving the house, and as I was waiting I gazed at one of the posters in the meditation center. It had a beautiful ocean image and a quotation from Baba that read, "You are never alone or helpless; the Force that guides the stars guides you too." While I was looking at the quotation, I started to compose a song expressing the idea that there is greatness within each one of us and that by remembering this we can overcome momentary sorrow and rise to tremendous accomplishments. I changed Baba's words a bit and entitled the song "We are Never Alone or Helpless."

It begins like this:

> *When the problems of the world lay heavy in your head*
> *And you don't know where to turn*
> *Why don't you go inside and find your inner strength*
> *And remember a lesson we must learn.*

Then the chorus comes in with Baba's words:

> *We are never alone or helpless, the force that guides the stars guides us too.*
> *We are never alone or helpless, the force that guides the stars guides us too.*

I started the composition while standing and waiting to go out of the house, but I was able to finish it later when I got back and picked up my guitar. In the late 1970s, a margi from the Philippines took this same phrase and incorporated it in a sweet spiritual tune. I, however, put the lyrics to a bouncy country-style melody. I performed it live with Brian at the Divine Moon Festival in England, and his fiddle part really fit well with the vibe of the song. On the New York recording, Ryan Sam turned it into a country-rock song with a driving beat and zesty piano and electric guitar backing.

A few years later I returned to this theme with a song entitled "From Zero to Hero." I got the idea from something I heard from one monk who recounted an experience he had had in India while representing Cairo sector in a reporting session with Baba. The other monks present there were asking him about the work he had done and he was not able to show much progress, in large part due to the difficulty in bringing a movement like Ananda Marga to conservative areas of the Middle East. Those monks started to criticize him and he felt bad. At that point, Baba intervened and said that one day Cairo sector will go "from zero to hero."

In another context, Baba once explained that if you put a 1 in front of a long string of zeros then it becomes a powerful number, and that 1 is Parama Purusha, the Supreme Consciousness.

I took this idea and wrote a song affirming that any moment we can turn a bad situation into something completely different, if we only remember our connection with the Supreme. The song begins with these lines:

> *Don't stay down, erase that frown*
> *Your present state, is not your fate*
> *There's more to you than you'll ever know*
> *Reach inside and let it show*

And then continues with the chorus-refrain:

> *From zero to hero you can make it if you try*
> *From zero to hero, grab some wings we're gonna fly*

I sent the finished lyrics to one of my colleagues whom I consider to be a great poet, and he encouraged me a lot by saying that this is the kind of song that can help people who are deeply depressed or even suicidal. His remark reminded me of a song that Billy Joel had written years earlier called "Second Wind," based on his personal struggle with depression and suicide.

I came up with a tune for the song and my first public performance of it was, fittingly enough, at a yoga studio in Cairo. When I performed the song for Ryan, he came back to me a week later with a rousing pop-rock-soul arrangement. I added my vocal part and soon we had a finished song for the CD.

There is another song on the *Love is the Best* CD entitled "Liberate Your Mind" that is frequently downloaded. This is a song in which I turn my attention to the problem of dogma and the restrictions that are placed on our minds in the religious, political, and social arenas of life.

The first lines of the song are as follows:

> *The preacher man says you're living in sin,*
> *A politician will do you in.*
> *How's a common man to win.*

The song continues with the refrain:

> *You've got to liberate your mind from fear*
> *The day of freedom is coming near*
> *Human life is very dear.*

As I thought of the song, especially the first line, I imagined that it would sound best gospel style, like in African-American churches. I told this to Ryan and he added a strong gospel piano accompaniment to the song. One day I would like to hear it performed by a gospel choir.

Another important song on this CD is "I'm Waiting for That Time." The song sums up what I would like to see happen in this world, what my dreams are for the future of humanity. Here are the lyrics of that song:

I'm waiting for that time, Yes, I'm waiting for that time.
I'm waiting for that time, Yes, I'm waiting for that time.
When good folks will hold their heads up high
When hungry kids will never pierce the night with their cry.
I'm waiting for that time, Yes, I'm waiting for that time.
I'm waiting for that time, Yes, I'm waiting for that time.
When we'll judge a man by what he does,
And not for who his father was...
When we'll love one another regardless of race,
And go pitch our tents in any old place...
When we'll share the earth's bounty fair and square,
And watch the world blooming everywhere...
I'm waiting for that time, Yes, I'm waiting for that time.
I'm waiting for that time, Yes, I'm waiting for that time.

Ryan came up with a sea-shanty arrangement for this song that speeds up frantically at the end and this is how we recorded it. In my public appearances I perform it as a Bob Dylan-style folk song.

The CD also includes a vegetarian song, a doo-wop bhajan, and a techno-trance rendition of the Baba Nam Kevalam mantra. All in all, it was a surprising departure from what might be expected from a musical monk.

After a few months of work, the CD was ready and I went on tour to promote it. I performed songs from this CD at the Ananda Marga retreat in Willow Springs, Missouri, and at the Prout Convention just outside of Copenhagen.

In August of 2009 I even had a feature performance at Luck Jack's. Instead of playing two songs at the open mic session of Mic Club, I was a featured performer with a full forty-five minute set. Ryan Sam came along and played keyboards and did backup vocals, and we performed all of the songs from the *Love is the Best* CD. This was the official CD release party and we had a full house that night. It was fun to do "Love is the Best" with everyone singing along and making the hand movements just like the kids at the kindergarten in Albania. Of course it was little bit different because some people had beer bottles in their hands when they lifted them high to say "Love is the Best."

"Love is the Best" at Mic Club on the Lower East Side of New York City.

Back to Brooklyn

Ever since I came back to the US, I thought that one day I should visit the old neighborhood in Brooklyn where I had spent the first nine years of my life but it took me a long time before I got around to doing it. Visiting the place where I grew up didn't seem to be a valuable use of my time; however, one day my curiosity got the best of me. I looked at the subway map and tried to figure out how I would get to East 96th Street in Brooklyn. It would have been possible to take a bus from Queens to Brooklyn, but it would have required taking a few buses with waiting times in between rides so I opted for the subway.

As the crow flies, Corona in Queens is only eleven miles from East Flatbush in Brooklyn, but the awkward layout of New York's subway system made it necessary to travel to Manhattan first and then change trains for Brooklyn, a trip that would take an hour and a half. I remembered that the closest subway stop to my old neighborhood used to be the East 98th Street station, but when I looked at the current subway map there was no such station. One station I did recognize was Sutter Avenue. I recalled

Sutter Avenue as a street with department stores, street vendors selling knishes (a tasty pastry filled with potatoes), and movie theaters. It was close to where my grandmother used to live and it was also within walking distance to where I wanted to go.

I got on the subway in Corona headed towards Manhattan, changed trains and was on my way to Brooklyn. The Sutter Avenue Station was not in good shape. It had an old worn-out look that was not helped by the graffiti on the walls. I got out and took my bearings and headed two blocks west along Rutland Road, another familiar street because we used to go to a bakery there that was dedicated to the production of bagels and bialys, an Eastern European soft, white savory pastry that has been called "the cousin to the bagel." I then turned south on 96th Street, walked two more blocks and finally stood in front of the building where I lived from 1946 to 1955.

It was a four-family, two-story brick building joined to a similar building on its left. The building looked the same, but it seemed to me that the trees on the street had changed. I remember thick foliage of strong sycamore trees whose roots were breaking the sidewalks. There were still some sycamore trees along the street but they were not as plentiful or as lush as I remembered them. I guess trees have their lifetime and life cycles too, and some of them may have been thinned out.

It was a hot summer day and there was no one out on the street. I walked to the corner of East 96th Street and Clarkson Avenue. This was an important intersection for me as a kid because it was the place where Little Lou's Luncheonette was located. The luncheonette had a long counter and a soda fountain and in the front by the cash register there were rows of chocolate and candies. We always used to call this place "the candy store" rather than a luncheonette, which was the big word the adults used. Like some of the sycamore trees, Little Lou's was no longer around. Instead there was a storefront church. In fact, there were several churches along Clarkson Avenue. These were churches of various African-American protestant denominations. When I left the area in the early 1950s, everybody there was Jewish and the only religious establishment on Clarkson Avenue was a storefront synagogue that finally moved to a large structure in 1955, just as my family was leaving the area.

An incident from 1952 best describes the ethnic makeup of this neighborhood during the early postwar era. Dwight Eisenhower was running for president against his Democratic opponent, Adlai Stevenson. Eisenhower was a war hero and he won the election in a landslide, but not in my old neighborhood. The night of the election my father came home in the late evening. He had been down at Little Lou's luncheonette, which also served as a polling station during elections, and apparently was able to find out how the vote went in that particular station. According to my father, Eisenhower didn't get a single vote. In those days Jewish-Americans voted solidly for the Democrats.

I didn't linger by the site of the old candy store but went a few blocks on Clarkson Avenue to my first elementary school, Public School 219. It had been given an additional name: Kennedy-King School. It was actually quite close to my old house but the distance seemed longer when I was growing up. School was out and I couldn't tell how it might have changed in the past fifty-five years, so I headed back to 96th Street. I was curious to know what had become of the big synagogue that was constructed in 1955, since there were no more Jews in the neighborhood. It was located only a block away from my old home and when I got there I found that it had been converted into an annex of Public School 219. It seemed to be a good use of the building.

I didn't have any big revelations from this excursion into the past, but my curiosity had been satisfied and I headed back to Queens.

I Move to the Midwest

There are some satiric maps with titles such as "The USA as Seen by a New Yorker" that show that for a New Yorker the only thing that is important is New York City and possibly California. The interior or Midwest of the United States is pictured on these maps as an empty or backward area. I had lived in Kansas in 1972 so I knew that there was something in the Midwest but I couldn't picture myself spending a lot of time there. That changed in September of 2009.

During a meeting with some other acharyas, someone suggested that I go to an Ananda Marga community in Illinois that needed a resident monk. The community was called Ananda Liina. It is a thirty-acre project located near the twin cities of Champaign-Urbana, about 130 miles south of Chicago. The margis there had constructed a yoga-meditation center, a sprout factory, an organic farm, a communal dining room and homes for individual families.

I visited and found it to be a very beautiful place. Though it was surrounded by corn fields, it was only a short drive to the nearby city, which was home to the largest campus of the University of Illinois. The community, with its own lake and forested areas, had the peace of the countryside but the convenience of a city. I really liked it and decided to move there.

Once I was settled, I enjoyed planting a vegetable garden again, and the yoga house where I lived was very comfortable. It was also a great place for small retreats and seminars. We held twice-yearly retreats for Ananda Margis from the Midwest and I gave local meditation instruction programs as well. In the summer time I conducted a Spiritual Lifestyle Training program, a two-week immersion course in meditation and yoga philosophy. I also held training sessions for Ananda Marga local full-time volunteers.

It's the System, Stupid, and a New CD

As was my wont, I also tried to find ways to perform and develop my music. At that time there were not as many open mic opportunities in Champaign and Urbana as there were in New York City. But in the small singer-songwriter get-togethers at a university coffee house I met a musician, Ron Cannon, who was able to help me produce another CD.

When I was putting together the *Love is the Best* album in 2009, I wanted to include more songs on it, but the producer wisely told me to save them for the next project. Though I liked the work that was done on the 2009 album, it was not exactly my style. I wanted something more in the vein of the folk, country and Americana genres. Ron Cannon was the perfect producer for this. He used to be the front man for a touring rockabilly band in the 1980s, and he was an exceptional guitarist and sound engineer.

Ron brought his recording equipment to the yoga house and we began work. One of the songs that I was eager to record was a song I had written in 2008. I had been listening to the BBC coverage of the US presidential election. Since I am not a big fan of conventional politics, an idea for a song popped into my mind. In 1992 Bill Clinton famously remarked, "It's the economy, stupid!" He ran his campaign on that slogan, saying that he was the candidate who would fix the economy. In 2008 I was sighing about the sameness of all the candidates vying for the presidential

nominations. I thought back to Clinton's remark, and said to myself, "Clinton didn't go far enough." He should have said, "It's the System, Stupid." The capitalist economic system is causing the problem, not the particular management style of one or the other parties.

I ran with this idea and wrote the song "It's the System, Stupid." Here are the original lyrics:

> *Everybody's wondering why the poor are getting poorer.*
> *Politicians saying that they giving more and morer.*
> *People scratch their heads while looking for a reason.*
> *If I tell you the answer, they may try me for treason.*
> *Chorus:*
> *It's the system stupid*
> *It's the system stupid.*
> *It's the system stupid.*
> *It's the system stupid.*
>
> *Tweedledee is running for election*
> *Tweedledum says he'll give us some protection.*
> *Nobody is getting to the root of the problems*
> *They're going round in circles, without a solution.*
> *It's the system, stupid......*
>
> *We're traveling together on a tiny green planet.*
> *Continue like this there'll be nothing left on it.*
> *It's time to stop the plunder, the greed and the looting.*
> *It's time for some healing, some caring and sharing.*
> *It's the system, stupid......*
>
> *You talk about raising the poor from the gutter*
> *But take a look around you at the fat cat's clutter.*
> *He can live without his Rolls Royce and luxury toys*
> *There will be enough for all, for all our girls and boys.*
> *It's the system, stupid......*

Without giving a big lecture about capitalism and US politics, I tried to make my views known in those four verses and in the chorus. I then sat down with my guitar and fitted the verses to a chord progression and "It's the System, Stupid" was born.

The song was written after my first CD and was part of the collection of unrecorded songs that I had available when I met Ryan Sam in New York in 2009. I wanted to put this song on the new CD that he was producing for me but when he heard it he said, "Dada, you will lose your audience if you record that song." I thought that perhaps his political stance was not as radical as mine. Since Ryan was not comfortable with the song, and since he had advised me to hold some songs in reserve for the next project, I kept this song off the *Love is the Best* album. But I still liked it a lot and wanted to record it. When I started working with Ron Cannon I asked him his opinion of this song. Ron had radical political ideas, so I did not think he would reject the song based on any bias. He listened to the song and didn't have any objections to recording it, but he gave me some good advice: "If you say, 'it's the system, stupid,' you are insulting the audience."

He had a good point. Not everyone remembered Bill Clinton's original comment. In fact, before performing the song in public I had to give a small talk explaining the context of the song and so on.

We were able to solve this problem by changing the line "It's the system, stupid!" to "It's the system, people!"

While we were in the process of recording the song, Steve, a margi drummer, came up with a reggae-style backbeat and the finished song became, in my opinion, one of the best on the album.

Another of my unrecorded songs which I wanted to put on the new CD was based on a spiritual poem by the Indian mystic Chaitanya Mahaprabhu (1486–1534). Chaitanya, best known for popularizing the Hare Krishna mantra and launching the kirtan movement in India, wrote a short poem giving powerful advice. He said:

> *Trnádapi suniicena taroriva sahisnuná;*
> *Amániná mánadena kiirtaniiyá sadá harih.*
> You must be more humble than the grass and as
> tolerant as a tree. You must give respect to those whom
> no one respects, and always do kiirtan of the Lord.

Baba used to give discourses based on these words and I thought that it would make a good song. I composed "Make Me Humble" with the following lyrics:

> *Look at everybody walking on the grass yet it pops up once again.*
> *It bears the steps and crushing weight without any end.*

I've got to be just as strong, you know I'm going to carry on.
So,
Make me humble like the grass
I'll be as tolerant as a tree
I'll give respect to all I see
I'll sing your name endlessly
Look at the trees giving everything, asking nothing in return.
Fruit and flowers for everyone, it's a lesson I'm gonna learn.
So,
Make me humble like the grass
I'll be as tolerant as a tree
I'll give respect to all I see
I'll sing your name endlessly
Look at everybody saluting the rich and the pretty ones too.
But take a look around you for that poor boy next to you.
Give him respect and dignity, it's the only thing we gotta do.
So,
Make me humble like the grass
I'll be as tolerant as a tree
I'll give respect to all I see
I'll sing your name endlessly
Oh Lord, you gave me a voice and I'm singing just for you.
I'm gonna sing every day and night, my whole life through.
So,
Make me humble like the grass
I'll be as tolerant as a tree
I'll give respect to all I see
I'll sing your name endlessly

I sang the main vocal on this song, but Ron added an Everly Brothers-style vocal harmony part that I really loved.

Another song that we worked on was a plea for peace based on a remark by the late Israeli Prime Minister Yitzhak Rabin, "Enough of blood, enough of tears," made after signing a peace accord with the Palestinians in 1993. That phrase became the start of my song "No More Blood, No More Tears" on which I made my first harmonica contribution to a recording.

The title song of the CD was "As the World Spins Around," a song that appeared on my very first CD in 2003. Why did I rerecord this song? First of all, I was not satisfied with how the first CD came out. I thought that many of the songs on it could be improved. But what really got me going was the response I received when I performed the song live in the various open mic venues. I usually used this as the opening song and often had the audience singing along with the easy "la, la, la, la" chorus.

At one venue in Brooklyn, the emcee loved the song so much, he always insisted that I come back on stage and do the song again. One time he even pressed me to do it a third time but I refused. After he accepted my refusal, he said, "That song is going to be a hit one day. I don't know how or when, but it will be a hit!" So we recorded the song again, hoping this would be the "hit version."

We worked on the CD bit by bit and Ron had me listen to some of the early versions of the recording. Local fiddle and mandolin players, margi women vocalists, a stand-up bass player, Steve, the margi drummer, and Ron with his guitar and hillbilly backing vocals all made great contributions to the final product. At first I was not sure how it would come out. I wondered whether Ron could really make everything sound right. However, when I listened to the final versions of the songs, I was highly satisfied. I named the CD *As the World Spins Around*. Quite a few people agreed with me that it was my best recording yet.

I did my best to promote it, sending it to some thirty radio stations. Some tracks were played on a few community and college radio stations around the country. Iowa Public Radio even played a live kirtan track from the album. The single "As the World Spins Around," has not yet become a hit as the emcee predicted, but I don't mind. I am proud to offer the song and the CD to anyone who wants to hear my music.

Do What You Can

While I was at Ananda Liina, my creative energies were directed into various channels. I began making audio and video recordings of my lectures and put these up on the Internet in the hopes of bringing our philosophy and practices to a wider public. I also performed music in social service venues for seniors and children with disabilities. Once a month I went to the Champaign County Nursing Home and played a mixture of old-time American songs, gospels, and a few of my own compositions.

At the Swann School, an institution in Champaign for children with disabilities, I performed a lot of the songs I had performed in the kindergarten in Albania. The only difference was that the children in the Swann School are severely disabled and it was hard for me to know whether the music was reaching them. The staff assured me that my music was helpful and kept inviting me back for more performances.

A weekly farmers market in Urbana provided another venue for my singing. Freed from the time limits of open mics, I played whatever I liked—a lot of my own songs, folk-rock songs from the 1960s, Americana and songs for kids. I noticed that I was getting a good response from the kids at the farmers market—in fact, some margi families said that their children really enjoyed listening to my CDs. I did not make my previous albums with children in mind but after seeing the response from the children at the farmers' market, I decided to make a CD of children's music.

Once I got this idea, I composed an original song based on a legendary story in the *Ramayana*. This epic poem describes an incident where Rama was building a bridge that was to stretch from India to the island of Sri Lanka where his wife, Sita, was held captive by his adversary Ravana. According to the story there were giant monkeys who were carrying huge stones, and even entire mountains, to help build the bridge. A small squirrel also wanted to help but could only carry pebbles to the bridge site. The little squirrel was humiliated by the monkeys, who belittled the squirrel's contributions. Rama came to the rescue, consoled the squirrel and stroked him on his back. And as everyone in India says, and as my song also proclaims, "That's why Indian squirrels have three stripes, ever since that day."

Since the story was already in the *Ramayana,* it was easy for me to write the lyrics to the song "Do What You Can," whose moral is we should work according to our capacity and not mind what others say about us. In addition, I had been listening to children's music and this helped me to create the right structure for the song, with lots of repetition.

After the song was written, I performed it at a retreat and it was well received. I also announced that I was going to make a CD for children. The problem was that I did not have other original songs to put on the CD so I stalled on the project. Then in the summer of 2013, I held a training session for Ananda Marga volunteers, and one of the trainees was a good musician who also had recording skills. We had a week on our hands before the training was to begin so we used that time to record "Do What You Can" as well as many of the songs that I had been singing with the kids in Albania and elsewhere over the past ten years. I rerecorded "Love is the Best," and the "Wise Ones Say," since these are good songs for children, and added Baba's "Tiny Green Island" as well as classic children's songs such as the "Eensy Weensy Spider." Before the week was finished, we had completed the album *Do What You Can*. The production is less sophisticated than my other albums, which took months to complete, but I also learned, like the title song says, that a small-sized effort is sometimes enough.

When someone first requested me to come to Ananda Liina in the Midwest I wondered whether this was the right move. I was not sure whether it would be an interesting place to live and work, but my initial misgivings were wrong. I have really enjoyed working from a base in the middle of America and wouldn't mind spending some more time here.

Epilogue

It is a hot day in the Midwest, the end of summer. The brilliant purple zinnias that I planted in late spring are beginning to fade. The tall, pink cosmos flowers waving in the wind next to the zinnias also look less glorious than they did two weeks ago. My garden is telling me, just as my calendar shows, that autumn will soon be at hand. As I think about this natural movement, I am reminded of the movement of my own life.

Not many people are born perfect, with all of their best traits intact. We develop our skills and good qualities over a lifetime, making lots of mistakes on the way. I wasn't born with a mystical bent of mind and an intense desire to render service to humanity. These are things which I worked on over my whole life, especially in the years since my first encounter with an Ananda Marga teacher.

A few years ago I did a mental exercise: If I could go back in the past, what would I do differently? My mind took a leap to the days when I was growing up. I pictured incidents where I caused pain to others by my words or deeds and thought: That is something I would change. I went through incident after incident, picturing how I would have handled a past situation with my present knowledge and state of being. After coming to the end of my list, I sat down for my normal meditation and felt great peace.

Not hurting others intentionally is just the first precept I learned in my encounter with the spiritual path, but when I did that little exercise I saw how the application of even this one bit of knowledge could have made a big difference in my life. Of course, in reality we can never go back and correct mistakes done in the past. We can only go on and vow to do better in the future. Baba repeatedly reminded us that our eyes have been placed in the front of our heads so that we can look ahead and not behind. He urged us to not only look ahead but to move towards our ultimate goal and take shelter in God.

This movement ahead towards yoga or union with the Supreme has kept me busy over the years. On top of that, my longing to help create a just and ideal society has also spurred me to move ahead without a pause. The calendar says that I should be in retirement by now. While the calendar informs my garden activities—I am busy planting some fall and winter vegetables—I do not pay it any heed when it comes to my larger plans. I intend to continue working. Hopefully I will die while working and work even while dying.

Over the years I have learned that whenever I acted in a way that brought me out of my comfort zone, it was then and there that I felt the help of the Cosmic Magician. I am not as adventurous as I was when I was barnstorming through France as a young monk giving lectures in city after city, day after day, but I am still active enough to expect and hope for a few more moments when I will again feel a divine wind pushing me onwards.

Acknowledgments

First of all, I am extremely grateful and indebted to my spiritual guide, Shrii Shrii Anandamurti, Baba. Without his guidance I would not have been able to write a memoir like this. My life would have undoubtedly taken another course. My acharya, Dada Yatiishvarananda, also helped me immeasurably to chart the path of my life.

I thank my colleague and friend Dada Nabhaniilananda for giving me the idea to start writing an account of my years on the spiritual path. Others who helped me include Dada Maheshvarananda, Ron Baseman, Amal Jacobson, and Donald Moore who all read the first drafts and gave valuable advice and suggestions for improvement. Many of the photos shown in the book were made available with the assistance of Tom Barefoot, who diligently manages the P.R. Sarkar Archives in Vermont. Rameshvar sent photos from my days in Poland and Shiila Serrano sent photos from France. Shaman Hatley provided expert assistance on Sanskrit usage. I also thank Randa Dubnick and Germaine Light for their proofreading. Devashish Donald Acosta did the final editing, proofreading and layout of the book, and I am deeply grateful for his expert guidance.

Lyrics for Donovan's "To Try for the Sun" © Peermusic Publishing.

The Casey Stengel quotes in chapter 1 are taken from the Senate Anti-Trust and Monopoly Subcommittee Hearing, July 8, 1958.

Glossary

Acharya (or acarya): Someone who teaches others by his or her conduct. A spiritual teacher. The monks and nuns of Ananda Marga hold the title acharya as do some lay members.
Anandamurti: Shrii Shrii Anandamurti is the founder and guru of Ananda Marga. Shrii is a title of respect. Anandamurti means "the image of bliss." His civil name was Prabhat Rainjan Sarkar. Disciples refer to him as Baba.
Ananda Sutram: The philosophical treatise of Ananda Marga.
Ananda: Unlimited bliss.
Ananda Marga: The path of bliss.
Ananda Marga Pracaraka Samgha: AMPS; the society to propagate the path of bliss; the formal name of Ananda Marga.
Ananda Nagar: The official headquarters of Ananda Marga, located in West Bengal. It is spread over several square miles and is home to schools and social service institutions run by Ananda Marga.
Ashram: A spiritual community; a place where a yogi lives.
Ashtanga yoga: The eight limbs of yoga.
Avadhuta (fem **Avadhutika**): An ascetic in the tantric tradition. Most of the monks and nuns of Ananda Marga are avadhutas and avadhutikas. They dress completely in orange and practice a special kind of meditation (kapalika sadhana).
Baba: The nearest and dearest one. The guru of Ananda Marga is lovingly addressed as Baba by his disciples.
Baba Nam Kevalam: "Only the name of the nearest and dearest one." The chanting mantra of Ananda Marga.
Bhajan: A spiritual song expressing love for God.
Bhukti Pradhan: Secretary of a district (bhukti).
Bhuta Shuddhi: Withdrawing the mind from attachment to outside physical surroundings; a process taught as part of the first lesson of Ananda Marga meditation.
Bhagavad Gita: The song of God; an Indian scripture in which philosophical

wisdom is presented in the form of a dialogue between a warrior (Arjuna) and his charioteer and guru (Krishna).

Brahmacarii: (Pronounced brah-ma-char-ee. Fem: brahmacarinii): One who remains connected with God. Monks in India are commonly called brahmacariis and in Ananda Marga novice monks and nuns have this title appended to their names.

Dada: Respected elder brother. The monks of Ananda Marga are referred to and addressed as Dada.

Darshan: Literally, to see. An occasion to see a guru is known as a darshan. Darshans are usually formal meetings in which disciples gather to listen to a teacher.

Dharma: Spirituality.

Dharmachakra (dharmacakra): The weekly collective meditation of Ananda Marga.

Dharma Maha Chakra (DMC): Literally, the great circle of spirituality; special spiritual congregations that were addressed by Baba during the years 1955–1990.

Dharma Samiksha: Review of dharma (spirituality); sessions in which Baba personally reviewed the conduct of devotees during the year 1981.

Didi: Respected elder sister. The nuns of Ananda Marga are referred to and addressed as Didi.

ERAWS: The Education, Relief and Welfare Section of Ananda Marga responsible for running schools, children's homes and other social projects.

Guru: The dispeller of darkness; a spiritual master or preceptor.

Half bath: An ablution before meditation; washing arms, legs and face.

Jagriti (pronounced ja-gri-tee): A place of spiritual awakening. The Ananda Marga centers are called jagritis.

Karma: Action; the law of action and reaction as applied to human life.

Kaoshiki: A yogic dance introduced by Shrii Shrii Anandamurti in 1978.

Kapalik: A tantric meditation process helping an aspirant to overcome fear.

Kiirtan (or **kirtan**): Chanting the name of God. The chanting is often accompanied by a dance.

Krishna or **Krsna**: A yogi and king who lived 3500 years ago. Krishna is viewed as a manifestation of God or a prophet by several religious traditions.

Kundalini: Spiritual energy that resides at the base of the spine and is elevated up the spinal column during the course of spiritual practice.

Kundalini yoga: Practices aimed at raising the kundalini.

Lungota: Yogic underwear worn by men.

Local Full Timer (LFT): Young men and women who work as full-time

volunteers for Ananda Marga, normally in their home countries.
Lungi: A sarong-like garment worn by men in India.
Mantra: Sounds or words that can liberate the mind. In meditation practice, mantras are repeated silently.
Margi: A member of Ananda Marga.
Master Unit: a rural social service and educational center of Ananda Marga
Microvita: Small living particles that straddle the line between matter and mind. The singular form is microvitum.
Neohumanism (also spelled **neo-humanism**): The social outlook of Ananda Marga. A spiritually and ecologically based version of humanism formulated by Baba in 1982.
Neohumanist education: Schools with a curriculum based on the values of neohumanism.
Parama Purusha: Supreme Consciousness; God.
PCAP: Prevention of Cruelty to Animals and Plants; the ecological department of Ananda Marga.
Prachar: Propagation, to spread; dharma prachar—spreading spirituality.
Pratik: The emblem of Ananda Marga consisting of an upward-pointing triangle, a downward-pointing triangle, a rising sun and a swastika. The pratik is worn by Ananda Marga members as a medallion over their chests, and the pratik is displayed in the books of Shrii Shrii Anandamurti and on the meditation altars in Ananda Marga centers.
Prout: Acronym for the progressive utilization theory. The social philosophy of Ananda Marga and the social and economic system described by that philosophy.
RAWA: Renaissance Artists and Writers Association.
RU: Renaissance Universal, a branch of Ananda Marga that publishes journals and organizes discussion on contemporary issues.
Samskara: The unexpressed reaction of a previous action or thought, commonly referred to as karma.
Samadhi: A state of trance-like absorption into the Cosmic Mind or Cosmic Consciousness. The eighth limb of classical yoga is samadhi.
Sadhana: Sustained effort. Spiritual practices, especially meditation, are called sadhana.
Sadvipra: A moral person who struggles for social justice.; an ideal leader with spiritual values.
Sectorial secretary: The overall supervisor of one of the nine Ananda Marga administrative sectors. The sectors usually comprise a continent or subcontinent and are named after a key city in that sector.

Sattvik (also spelled **sattvic**): Pure or sentient.
Shiva: The codifier of Tantra. He lived in India, 5000 BCE.
Shloka: A Sanskrit poem usually expressing a spiritual or philosophical idea.
Sutra: A Sanskrit aphorism.
Tantra: The practice that liberates a person from worldly bondage through expansion.; one of the original spiritual traditions of India out of which yoga emerged.
Tandava: The jumping dance of Shiva that builds courage and mental concentration.
Trikuti: Literally, three hills; the yogic concentration point located between the two eyebrows.
Varabhaya Mudra: A blessing that provides protection and removes fear.
Whole Time Workers, Whole Timers, WT: Monks and nuns working full-time for Ananda Marga.
Yoga: The union of individual consciousness with Cosmic Consciousness; the physical, mental and spiritual practices that are employed to reach union with Cosmic Consciousness.

www.ingramcontent.com/pod-product-compliance
Lightning Source LLC
Chambersburg PA
CBHW021101080526
44587CB00010B/332